*blacker
than
thou*

blacker than thou

the struggle for campus unity

by
GEORGE NAPPER
Spelman College

WILLIAM B. EERDMANS PUBLISHING COMPANY
Grand Rapids, Michigan

Library of Congress Cataloging in Publication Data

Napper, George, 1939–
Blacker than thou.

Based on the author's thesis, University of
California, Berkeley, 1970.
Bibliography: p.
1. Negroes—Education (Higher).   2. Negroes—
Race identity.   3. Black power—United States.
I. Title.
LC2781.N36 1973   378.1'98'1   72-96404
ISBN 0-8028-3427-2
ISBN 0-8028-1524-3 (pbk.)

230833

To the memory of Mama
who struggled relentlessly for her family

For Chee, Kendall, and Kenya

and

For Liz

Stop!

Black student after winter vacation on his way back to school (University of America) a part of the Jet set. I wouldn't have noticed him, but he was dressed rather oddly; along with about a five-inch natural he had an Indian band around his forehead; with a gold ear-ring in his left ear. A black tiki hung around his neck partially hid under a red and green scarf that loosely covered an orange dashiki that housed a black turtle neck sweater. His tailor-made white bell bottoms were accented by brown buckled cowboy boots while a black slick-haired fur coat rested on his right arm looking like it could bite. Now, here we have a brother that didn't know what he was, an international nigger—you name it, he'll be a part of it. As I approached him, his first words after "What's happnin, baby," were "Do you smoke, bro."

Stop!

Time is not new; it must be on our side, we're still here. Send young black brothers and sisters to college and they come home Greeks, talking about they can't relate to the community anymore. So here we have black Alpha Phi Alpha, Delta Sigma Theta, etc., unable to speak Greek, with an obvious non-knowledge of Greek culture—only supported by an ignorance of their own past (or present); only, after four years, to be graduated as some of the best whist players since the Cincinnati Kid who didn't finish high school.

—Don L. Lee, *We Walk the Way of The New World*

preface

In the study of social movements, there is a dictum: "No movement is as coherent as it appears from without; no movement is as incoherent as it appears from within." It is particularly true in the early stages that members seem to be not only united, but held together by a single dimension of experience, thought, and commitment. The early Christians had only one public version of themselves, and there were good reasons for the question, "Are you a Christian or aren't you?" and not, "What kind of a Christian are you?" A lot of time went by before the salient categories became Protestant or Catholic, Huguenot or Methodist, German Lutheran or Irish Catholic.

Similarly and more recently, the early communists had only one public version, and some time and successes passed before the important categories became Stalinist or Trotsky-ite or Maoist, or the Cuban version versus the Yugoslavian, Czech, or Vietnamese versions.

When this book was begun, we were in the very earliest stages of the Black Power movement in the United States. There was the ideal of only one version of blackness presentable to the outside world, and those assuming the leadership defined its substance and manner of expression. In this framework, it makes sense that the important question became, "Are you black or aren't you?" and not, "What kind of black are you?" Among the many functions of a single dimension of experience and its single legitimate mode of expression are the closing of ranks, the identification of members and sympathizers, the development of a

[7]

sense of solidarity, and the portrait of a united front. But as in every movement, the early affirmation of a single unity also preempts a consideration of an alternative unity. Here, many will always find themselves in the double-bind. For those blacks who wanted to see serious and radical social change, but who were not in support of the particular content of black unity presented at any given moment, there was the unfortunate option of either appearing "not black" by refusing to publicly support the leadership, or equally unfortunate, of backing the leadership and its rhetoric publicly without the personal commitment to sustain any long-term political support. (One result was that black "leaders" could get hung out on the long limb of their own rhetoric, lulled and deluded by the incantation of the equally rhetorical supportive response.)

Generally true for blacks located formally as equals in predominantly white institutions, nowhere was this truer than for black students in predominantly white universities of the period. For thousands of these students in 1968-69, whether at Cornell or Northwestern, Harvard or Yale, Antioch or Oberlin, Michigan or Illinois, San Francisco State or Berkeley, this double-bind was a near universal. Those who participated* in that year's revolt will find themselves somewhere among these pages of George Napper's account. For while he gives vivid descriptions of the actual setting at Berkeley, Napper generates enough of an abstracted understanding of the patterns of the conflict so that a student from Massachusetts can find his mirror-image in some section of this book. It should therefore not be read as a book about California, or another of those timely monographs on the topic of student violence in the sixties, but as an analysis of movement strife, process, and development.

I would like to anticipate three likely criticisms of the work, and in addressing each of them, point to what I see as the general value of the study. The first criticism is political,

* It was very difficult to avoid some kind of active political participation, since either going to class as usual or staying away was interpreted as a political statement. Participation was at least psychically political.

[8]

the second analytic or conceptual, the third is a combination. I will list them, and turn to them in reverse order.

First, some are likely to claim that Napper is ripping the covers off and revealing individual differences among blacks at a time when the appearances of black unity are required. Second, the use of the categories of colonization is likely to come under attack by those critics generally impatient with the application of this model to the black situation in the United States, and specifically to an account of relatively privileged black youth. Finally, there is a growing impatience with research of any kind on the black movement, especially among those inclined to argue that we already know enough; that the problem is simply to act.

It is partly true that we "already know enough" about the situation of blacks in the United States. We already know that blacks have occupied the largest rung at the base of the U.S. labor market and political structure for the last two hundred years. We knew that eighty years ago. In that sense, we have long known enough, and we don't need more research to locate the condition of blacks for the purpose of finding out if things ought to be changed.

We also know that social change is as much a result of external and extrinsic forces as that of deliberate collective action, but there is room for considerable humility about what the relationship or balance is. For example, we simply do not know enough about the conditions under which blacks or any group will submerge individual differences and conflicting personal or class interests for the sake of the larger collectivity. To say that "all we have to do is unite as a people and move to a common destiny" is as true as it is tired and useless.

We need to know more about how conflicting loyalties and conflicting identities are translated into (or diverted from) the solitary purpose that I mentioned at the outset. Napper's third chapter provides some good case material on this problem, and those interested in the creation and sustenance of movement unity can profit from a close reading. We also need some fresh analysis of actual conflict situations that tries to escape the rhetorical posturing. This leads me

[9]

to my second point, the anticipation of the critical response to the use of the model of colonialism. It seems to me that the critical question to be asked about the model is *how* it is used, not whether or not it is valid.

The purpose of using a metaphor or an analog is not to demonstrate that one situation is exactly like another. It hardly takes skill or insight to point out the differences between two different situations. The metaphor, the analogy, or the application of some more general formulation should function to excite the imagination to think of new similarities between different situations. In literature, the unlikely metaphor can be compelling when it focuses attention on parallels that we otherwise would not have conceived. In the social sciences and history, the attempt to apply a general formulation can have a similar function. We can be jostled into thinking of further parallels along the line indicated by the formulation.

That I see as Napper's purpose in the use of Memmi, Blauner, and others who have used the model of colonialism, and it is one of his contributions to add flesh and sinew to the skeleton. His conclusion is no simplistic rhetorical flourish that states that "black students are colonized." Instead, his detailed account of some of the parallels may suggest to some that there are even more similarities that we would otherwise have ignored.

Finally, there is the question of unity and its appearances, and the social and political function of portraying differences. Good men can and will disagree about this matter. It is an open question, and to attempt to foreclose it by fiat is both foolish and temporary. The reason is simple, for there is a piece of truth on both sides. On the one hand, it is possible to create stronger bonds by asserting the requirements of unity, de-emphasizing differences. But there are unseen and dangerous pitfalls to a strategy that forges a public unity that is not sufficiently experienced for the purpose of collective action. Disillusionment, contempt, and withdrawal are far heavier losses to a movement than factionalism. I hinted at the beginning that the dilemma is best settled by looking at timing and social context. It is my

[10]

view that events of the last few years indicate that we have reached a propitious time for an *open* analysis of the nature of unity and of the possible different paths that can be taken in the name of that unity. The seeds of such analysis are all around us; this book is one of them, and I hope that it encourages other works of its kind.

Troy Duster
University of California,
Berkeley

contents

[13]

acknowledgments

I wish to express my gratitude to the Center for the Study of Law and Society of the University of California at Berkeley for the generous financial and clerical support provided me while I was initially preparing this work for a dissertation. My gratitude is also extended to the members of my dissertation committee, Professors Andrew Billingsley, Paul Takagi, and especially Troy Duster for encouragement and critical guidance.

I owe a special thanks to the Spelman College Faculty Development Committee for a grant allowing me time to prepare the manuscript for publication. I also wish to thank Mrs. Juanita Kirby and Mrs. Helen Johnson for the conscientiousness they demonstrated with the typing.

To Mrs. Roseann Bell, my dear friend and colleague, I am deeply and warmly indebted for her provocative editorial assistance. It is difficult to imagine how this work would have been completed without her.

My wife Chee, my children Kendall and Kenya (to whom this book is dedicated), have been specially associated with the preparation of this book. They shared, with love and understanding, the joys and pains I experienced in researching and writing the manuscript.

Finally, I wish to thank the black students at the University of California at Berkeley who so graciously shared with me their time, their thoughts, and the agonies and ecstasies of their experiences as black students on a predominantly white campus. Without them this book could not have been written. I trust that my interpretation in this work does justice to them and provides them and other black college students with a basis for more informed action in their continued struggles.

introduction / 1

This book examines the political world of the black college student and analyzes his registration of preferences in the milieu of predominantly white institutions of higher learning. Specifically, the book introduces a new perspective on student unrest during the Black Student Movement.

What has become known as the Black Student Movement in this country germinated in an exquisite set of events sloganized as "Black Power." The rise of the Black Power Movement in the middle of the 1960's generated a change in the political outlook of black people. The outlook changed from one that was integrationist-assimilationist to one extolling the virtues of black nationalism and black separatism. The Movement gained momentum following the death of Dr. Martin Luther King, Jr., in April 1968, and its validity was corroborated by black student activities which assumed national proportions in the academic year 1968-69.

During that year, a great number of college campuses in this country were swept with a wave of strikes and demonstrations, many of which were led and organized by black students. From picket lines, sit-ins, and boycotts to class disruptions, the seizure of buildings, and shotgun showdowns, black students, in part, brought the struggle to the halls of academia.

The demands the students brought to the attention of the status-quo administrators and faculties of those predominantly white institutions spoke in wholesale form to the need for the universities to become more responsive to human needs, and to incorporate perspectives and values

[15]

outside the one-dimensional premise of the "superiority" of Anglo-Saxon Western culture. The students' particular demands addressed the need to have black values reflected at every level of the academic experience—in curriculum changes, in faculty and administrative changes, and in the involvement of greater proportions of students who come from backgrounds traditionally excluded from the university experience.

The protests of black college students must be seen within the framework of the historical black adventure in this country. They are part of the black struggle for freedom and dignity. We must properly examine and understand the forces that have shaped the black experience generally if we are to understand the political world of the Black Student Movement in particular.

In a profound sense it is important to know and acknowledge (1) that American society is and always has been rigged *against* blacks and *for* whites; and (2) that these same mechanisms have been stacked in favor of those whites who are classified as "Haves"; it is this group that is primarily responsible for the rigging itself. In the academic setting this disparity is shown in virtually all-white faculty and administrative appointments, all-white-centered curricula, all-white theoretical models, etc. The particular niche that black people have in this "game" and the nature of race relations of which this "scheme" is a part have been substantially documented and articulated as part of the colonial model.[1]

Basically the model states that the colonizer (the European) has imposed his value system and institutions upon the colonized (the non-European—and in this case the black). By way of oppressing and exploiting the colonized, and by creating a racist ideology to both maintain and rationalize his position of superiority, the colonizer has

---

[1] The colonial model as an explanatory concept is presented and elaborated upon in Stokely Carmichael and Charles V. Hamilton, *Black Power* (New York: Random House, 1967); Kenneth B. Clark, *Dark Ghetto* (New York: Harper & Row, 1965); Robert Blauner, "Internal Colonialism and Ghetto Revolt," *Social Problems,* XVI, No. 4 (Spring 1969); Albert Memmi, *The Colonizer and the Colonized* (Boston: Beacon Press, 1967).

effectively precluded the participation of the colonized in the mainstream of the affairs of the society. In all his decisions, the colonizer attempts to determine and constrain the destiny of the colonized.

Thus, there are two dimensions to this model that are of importance here. First, there is the overt, objective dimension which can be seen in the lopsided power relationships in every sphere of life in this society between blacks and whites. Whites determine and control the nature of economics and politics, as well as the "legitimate" arena of violence. For the most part this is true whether one speaks of geographic areas occupied predominantly by whites, or predominantly by blacks.

The other dimension of colonialism is more covert and subjective, and for the purposes of this study it is the more important of the two dimensions. This dimension concerns itself with culture and the processes of socialization. It therefore deals more with psychological exploitation than it does with the more measurable aspects of economic, physical, and political exploitation. The colonizers (whites in America) use their culture (as well as exploiting that of the colonized blacks in America) to socialize the colonized into an identification with white values—to control blacks, to make them carbon copies of whites, and, therefore, to preserve the status quo.

Albert Memmi, whose writings on the colonial situation are remarkable for their clarity and insight, captures the essence and the end goal of this process when he writes:

> The colonized does not seek merely to enrich himself with the colonizer's virtues. In the name of what he hopes to become, he sets his mind on impoverishing himself, tearing himself away from his true self. [Therefore] the first ambition of the colonized is to become equal to that splendid model (the colonizer) and to resemble him to the point of disappearing in him.[2]

Memmi's words describe the colonizer's objectives. They also point out the obstacles that must be effectively dealt

2 *The Colonizer and the Colonized,* p. 121.

[17]

with by blacks to bring about significant changes in this society. Such a task is indeed formidable, for all is weighted against its being accomplished. W. E. B. DuBois was able to see the larger context of this problem, namely the attempts of black people to come to grips with the contradictions of being black in white America:

> . . . The Negro is a sort of seventh son, born with a veil, and gifted with second sight in this American world—a world which yields him no true self-consciousness, but only lets him see himself through the revelation of the other world. It is a peculiar sensation, this sense of always looking at one's self through the eyes of others, of measuring one's soul by the tape of a world that looks on in amused contempt and pity. One ever feels his two-ness—an American, a Negro; two souls, two thoughts, two unreconciled strivings; two warring ideals in one dark body, whose dogged strengths alone keep it from being torn asunder . . . the history of the American Negro is the history of this strife. . . .[3]

The impact of this double-consciousness has been heightened for black people by the onset of the Black Power Movement. For the black college student, especially if he is on a predominantly white campus, the impact has been particularly great. His position in the strata of American society has been defined in terms of being alienated and socialized away from the black community towards identification with the values and norms of white middle-class America. Now that identification is being challenged by the cries of the Black Power Movement to "return home." While the cries have a reality of their own, their existence, unlike that of a magic wand, does not sweep the boards clean. The return home has its obstacles and barriers. Nonetheless, the trek has begun.

I would like to suggest that the best way to understand the plight of the black college student is to see him stationed between the pull of two poles. On the one hand are the norms and values of white middle-class America, and on

3 W. E. B. DuBois, *The Souls of Black Folks* (New York: Fawcett World Library, 1965), pp. 16-17.

the other are the counter-values and norms of the emerging black community as articulated by militant black nationalists. Thus, the black student is caught in the throes of role conflict.[4] This book deals with how this conflict is handled by the black college student as a political actor.

Accordingly, we seek to examine three questions: (1) What are the general terms and conditions that generate the conflict situation for the black college student? (2) How does he seek to resolve the conflict within the context of his socio-political world? and (3) What are the consequences of his attempt to resolve the conflict for black unity and the Black Student Movement?

In the chapter that follows, "The Politics of Becoming Black," I consider the impact of the Black Power Movement for black college students, the conflict that evolved, and the socio-political types that emerged from it.

In the third chapter, "The Struggle to 'Get It Together': The Strike at Berkeley," I critically explore the terms and conditions that led to the strike at Berkeley, and the strike's larger implications for black unity on predominantly white campuses.

Chapter Four, "Black Man, Black Woman: 'Them Changes,' " examines the relationship between black men and black women and factors affecting "the changes" they suffer and enjoy from each other. Further the relationship of these unnatural foes is scrutinized in view of the establishment and sustenance of unity within the Black Student Movement.

Chapter Five summarizes and discusses the dimensions of this book's findings for the struggle for unity in the Black Student Movement.

The final chapter of the book, "Addendum: Gettin' Over," assesses what is going on now and why in the socio-political world of black college students.

---

[4] The importance of this concept is not limited to explaining the black political behavior of individuals. It also has its organizational dimensions. See Inge Powell Bell, *CORE and the Strategy of Nonviolence* (New York: Random House, 1968); or Nicholas Alex, *Black in Blue: A Study of the Negro Policeman* (New York: Appleton-Century-Crofts, 1969).

A Note on Terminology

Throughout this work the terms "whiteness" and "blackness" occur. When I use "whiteness" in the most general sense, I am referring to the whole cultural value system on which Western society is based.

More specifically, I am referring to the white middle-class model (or "materialist-success syndrome")—which uses indices such as occupation, size of home, style of life, and size of income to assess the worth of an individual—along with the standards of good, evil, and beauty that emanate from this model. We speak, then, of the culture and values of the white middle class in America as "whiteness."

"Blackness" will be used to denote the culture of the black lower class, because this class embraces the overwhelming majority of black people in this country and because it is within this milieu that styles of life and characteristics distinctively "black" find their greatest expression.

Further, "blackness" represents the emphasis that is placed on being a "street Nigger" (an updating of the "field Nigger" concept in the field Nigger-house Nigger distinction).[5] I use this frame of reference as an anchor because the development of a black ethos and a definition of blackness apart from this context are still in the making and await a more specific description.

It is instructive to point out that I use such words as

---

[5] Malcolm X attributes the origins of this distinction to the stratification processes which took place during slavery:

There were two kinds of slaves, the house Negro and the field Negro. The house Negroes—they lived in the house with the master, they dressed pretty good, they ate good. . . . They loved the master more than the master loved himself. . . . If the master's house caught on fire, the house Negro would fight harder to put the blaze out than the master would. If the master got sick, the house Negro would say "What's the matter, boss, we sick?" And if you came to the house Negro and said "Let's run away, let's escape, let's separate," the house Negro would look at you and say, "Man, you crazy, what you mean separate? Where is there a better house than this?"

On that same plantation, there was the field Negro—those were the masses. The Negro in the field caught hell. He ate leftovers. In the house they ate high "attitude" and "atmosphere" in connection with "blackness" to capture the world of the black college student on the predominantly white campus, in distinction from that part of the black community used by these students as the point of reference for emulation (the "street-Nigger" segment). For some readers such a distinction is artificial because, as they would argue, the wretched conditions of racism and the realities of being black are the same for all blacks regardless of one's station in American society. A "Nigger" student is viewed by white society as being a "Nigger" as much as any other black person. Despite the political usefulness of this statement for black unity, however, the realities of college life for black students are not the realities of life for most residents of the larger black community. The "street-Nigger" roles (pimp, hustler, gangster, etc.) that many of the community inhabitants play are governed by a fight for survival that does not permit a moving in and out of these roles at will. Too frequently social conditions imposed on the black community create these roles and force many of the residents to have their personalities and behavior patterns confirmed in them.

Many black college students have taken the life of the street Nigger as a model for their own life style. The emulation of these roles under conditions remarkably different from those originating and sustaining them suggests their artificiality. The *attitude* of those students who act out such roles and the *atmosphere* in which the drama takes place can only be approximations of the real thing.

---

on the hog. The field Negro was beaten from morning to night; he lived in a shack, in a hut. . . . He hated his master, he was intelligent, when the house caught on fire, he didn't try to put it out; that field Negro prayed for a wind, for a breeze. When the master got sick, the field Negro prayed that he'd die. If someone came to the field Nigger and said, "Let's separate, let's run," he didn't say, "Where are we going?" He'd say, "Any place is better than here!" You've got field Negroes in America today. I'm a field Negro. The masses are the field Negroes. When they see this man's house on fire, you don't hear the little Negroes talking about "our government is in trouble," they say, "the government is in trouble."—*Malcolm X Speaks,* ed. George Breitman (New York, 1966), pp. 11-12.

A Note on Methods

This study came about as a result of my accepting employment as the associate to the Assistant Chancellor for Academic Affairs at the Berkeley campus of the University of California. I was urged to enter this capacity by fellow members of the Afro-American Students Union, due principally to the role I played in helping to write a proposal submitted by the Afro-American Students Union to the Chancellor of the Berkeley campus for the creation of a Black Studies Department. One of my primary responsibilities was to help develop and implement the central nexus that the proposal contained.

While I was in the employ of the University I gave active support to the strike which was called in January 1969, for the reason that was stated as the cause in striking—to effect a Black Studies Department. (The strike is discussed in detail in Chapter III. There I make a distinction between reasons stated and other unstated reasons precipitating the strike.) Although I frequently took issue with certain aspects of the implementation of the strike, the stated reasons for calling it were accepted as morally, politically, and socially correct. Thus, I participated in many activities of the strike, including picketing, mounting strike support, attending and negotiating in sessions with the administration of the University, and writing proposals and other documents designed to achieve the announced purpose of the strike. Activities like the latter tied into what I perceived as part of my job responsibilities. So the role of associate to the Assistant Chancellor for Academic Affairs became one that actively supported the announced purposes of the strike, a role that was not always in harmony with the Chancellor's expectations.

It was during the strike period, while attending dozens of various meetings each week with black students, and while talking to black students individually and in small groups, that I became sensitized to the fact that there were factors operating within the ranks of the black student population that were detrimental to the goal of black unity. I began to see numerous subtle and overt developments that thwarted the unanimity of feeling that one might expect to exist in such a meaningful undertaking as fighting for a Black Studies Department. The strike, then, and my active participation in it, afforded me a perspective and insight that formed the basis for the interviews that were later conducted. My observations and concerns led to the writing of this book.

The forty students interviewed for this study (though fewer are actually cited here) were students at the Berkeley campus of the University of California.[6] All of the respondents (referred to by "R" followed by a number reflecting the order in which they were interviewed), with the exception of one, were participants in the strike activities. Their activities ranged from picketing, leafleting, and making speeches to behavior that involved acts labeled as "rule breaking" by the Administration. Some in this category were caught and arrested, others were expelled or suspended. All black students on campus were not involved in strike activities and many of them, therefore, continued to go to classes. Others were not actively involved, but their inaction—i.e., staying away from campus—made them *ipso facto* strikers whether they were committed to the announced ends of the strike or not. Many others participated in strike activities but continued going to classes.

The actual selection of respondents was based on names made available by sign-up sheets that were used by various committees formed during the strike. By and large, these names indicated those active in one way or another in strike activities. These students were phoned and informed of the author's interest in interviewing them to get their attitudes about a number of relevant issues, including the strike. The overwhelming majority were favorable to the idea. Those who made and kept appointments were interviewed. Four of the forty students interviewed came from the leadership ranks.

Each interview was guided by open-ended questions that were formulated on an interview schedule and recorded on a

6 A profile of the students interviewed is contained in the Appendix.

tape recorder. All respondents were aware of the presence of the tape recorder, and each respondent gave his approval for the tape recorder's being used.

While rapport is no substitute for skills needed in interviewing, the fact that I am black and had gained some exposure by being active in the strike probably made it easier for me to share conversations with the respondents. The need for many of them to talk about their feelings in an atmosphere of privacy was probably another factor contributing to the smoothness of the interview sessions.

But before turning to the specific dynamics of black student unrest, it is necessary to take a look at the broader context of black politics in the 1960's.

the politics of becoming black   *II*

> We then witness a reversal of terms. Assimilation being aban-
> doned, the colonized's liberation must be carried out through a
> recovery of self and of autonomous dignity. Attempts at imitat-
> ing the colonizer required self-denial; the colonizer's rejection is
> the indispensable prelude to self-discovery. That accusing and
> annihilating image must be shaken off; oppression must be
> attacked boldly since it is impossible to go around it. After
> having been rejected for so long by the colonizer, the day has
> come when it is the colonized who must refuse the colonizer.[1]

The decade of the 1960's assumes a special importance
for my task in this study. It is a period that witnessed the
abrupt displacement of a political and psychological commitment to the assimilationist-integrationist ideal by an
equally compelling conformity to a swiftly unfolding black
ideal that brought a plethora of identity problems and other
related complications. This era can be viewed as reflecting
two political periods characterizing the politics of black
people. One period can be referred to as the "pre-Black
Power period," and the other, the "Black Power period."

It is difficult for one to determine with precision when
the politics of integration in the pre-Black Power period
deferred to its antithesis, the politics of blackness, reflecting
the arrival of the Black Power period. On the one hand it
can be argued that the Black Power period began with the
wave of disturbances in urban areas in 1963 and 1964—
demonstrations which reflected the irrelevance of the con-

---

1   Albert Memmi, *The Colonizer and the Colonized,* p. 178.

[25]

cept of integration for many blacks at the bottom rung of the ladder. A strong sympathy for Black Power pre-dated its emergence on the national front as a slogan and rallying cry for a growing number of black people. Or one can use the Meredith march through Mississippi in June 1966 as the beginning point. If the former is used as the starting point, then the Meredith march was merely a reflection of moods already being generated in the black community. Notwithstanding the lack of unanimity among the leaders of the march regarding the slogan "Black Power" and the outright disapproval of its usage by some of the leaders, I see the march as the catalyst for the launching of Black Power.[2]

It was during this march that the slogan received a national forum. The feelings of seething anger, frustration, and alienation in black urban areas were verbally and emotionally harnessed in a slogan that embraced the black interests of the areas' inhabitants.

The pre-Black Power period and its successor are chiefly distinguished by their orientation to the concept of integration as a meaningful goal for black people in white America. The politics of the pre-Black Power period sought integration wholeheartedly as a goal for black people, as the only way black people could gain justice, freedom, and equality in this country. The price of achieving these ends, however, was the sacrifice of one's blackness. This issue became a primary target for those who became the chief architects of Black Power because of the failure of integration to keep its promise. Both the price and the failure of integration ushered in the Black Power period. Stokely Carmichael, one of those most closely identified with the Black Power Movement, responded to integration in the following manner in 1966:

> . . . Integration speaks not at all to the problem of poverty, only to the problem of blackness. Integration today means the man who "makes it," leaving his black brother behind in the

[2] The leaders decided that the concept was not to be used as the official slogan of the march, irrespective of the national notoriety the slogan was receiving.

ghetto as fast as his new sports car will take him. It has no relevance to the Harlem wino or to the cotton-picker making three dollars a day. . . .

Integration, moreover, speaks to the problem of blackness in a despicable way. As a goal, it has been based on complete acceptance of the fact that *in order to have* a decent house or education, blacks must move into a white neighborhood or send their children to a white school. This reinforces in both black and white the idea that "white" is automatically better and "black" is by definition inferior. This is why integration is a subterfuge for the maintenance of white supremacy.[3]

Again in 1967:

The concept of integration had to be based on the assumption that there was nothing of value in the Negro community and that little of value could be created among Negroes, so the thing to do was to siphon off the "acceptable" Negroes in the surrounding middle class community.[4]

The politics of the pre-Black Power period was characterized by an unconditional acceptance, consciously or unconsciously, of the notion of white superiority and the white-oriented values of this society. Thus, the goal of that movement was to be "let in," to be assimilated. This being the case, the tendency in self-identification was to stress, psychologically, the whiteness of one's total makeup and to degrade or dismiss one's "blackness."

Like the black middle class of which it is a part, the audience to which the pre-Black Power black college student responded and to which its attitudes and interests were oriented was that of the white establishment. This orientation was a result of the profound impact of white cultural values on the formation of black thought and self-perception. The impact is well documented and is found in such

3 "Power and Racism," *The Black Power Revolt,* ed. Floyd Barbour (Toronto: Macmillan, 1968), pp. 68-69.

4 Robert L. Scott and Wayne Brockriede, *The Rhetoric of Black Power* (New York: Harper & Row, 1969), p. 105.

sayings in the black community as, "If you're white, you're alright; if you're brown, stick around; but if you're black, get back." This is not only a realistic social assessment, but more importantly (and of more devastating impact on the development of black people) it is a value judgment having powerful suggestions for self-perception.

To call someone "black" was a pejorative of the highest degree. It was a fighting word. To have thick lips or nappy hair was the height of ugliness. When a black person was referred to as being "tough" or "foxy" (handsome, pretty, good-looking), there was no real possibility that the person could have any of those qualities. To be black was to be crude, to be loud, or to manifest any of the stereotypes attributed to black people—e.g., having rhythm or liking the color red. Exhibiting these stereotypes was to be avoided, especially near white people, and at all times for those having self-respect. The dynamic black poet Don Lee tersely captures the feeling of being referred to as black during the pre-Black Power period:

> like
> if he hadda called me
> black seven years ago,
> i wd've . . .
>   broke his right eye out,
>   jumped into his chest,
>   talked about his momma
> lied on his sister
>   & dared him to say it again
> all in one breath . . .
> seven years ago.[5]

It is against this setting that one can gauge the powerful importance of such contemporary slogans as "Black is beautiful" for black people in white America. Further, it is against this backdrop that one can appreciate the problems of the black middle class and of black college students aspiring to become middle class, facing up to the reality that

---

5 Don L. Lee, *Don't Cry, Scream* (Detroit: Broadside Press, 1969), p. 12.

they too are black. It is a reality dramatized by the sudden appearance of a perspective opposed to that to which the black middle class and black college students had historically been politically and psychologically committed.

Black students attending college during the Black Power period understand that their location in this society affords them privileges and liberties that are not forthcoming to their brothers in the streets and ghettos. Indeed, it is because of this sensitive awareness that an atmosphere of conflict, contradiction, and guilt competes with the students' commitments in playing their role, a role which is increasingly seen by them as the product of having been plucked away from the "community" and its harsh realities and brought to the "Big House" to enjoy its fruits and riches. The black college student understands that his status has changed from that of a "field slave" to that of a "house slave," with the increased privileges and the stature that accompany this transition.

At a time when black nationalism, black pride, and the survival of the black experience have been given high priority by those forces that now dominate the black political arena, the conventional thinking among today's young black intellectuals and college students is that they are involved in a socialization process that is designed, and has been historically designed, to take them away from their black heritage and place them within a "sea of whiteness" that is hermetically sealed off from those conditions that characterize the plight of their brothers in the streets. Thus higher education has become defined as an insidious tool of the white man, and the realities of the campus community are seen in stark contrast to the realities of life in the ghetto.

In the days before Black Power and the special programs of higher education for blacks, the question of black students' proceeding along assimilationist-integrationist sanctioned avenues of success, using education as the primary vehicle, was never a real issue. The white values and patterns of behavior dictated by institutions of higher education were accepted without question by blacks on college campuses. They quickly learned to shed the characteristics and life styles that were labeled "black"—if they had them—and embrace a white perspective of the world.

The intent here is not to excoriate these students or to be harsh with them by benefit of the standards and ideologies that prevail today. Rather, it is important to point out the conditions of that time and the values that existed in contrast to what is going on now as a way of trying to clarify how, in fact, conditions have changed today's black students on white campuses.

Not that the shift from a white orientation to a black orientation, from integration to black nationalism, has been consummated. What has been provided is a process of transition to accomplish the change. This process has created for black college students in general, and those on white campuses in particular, a situation that is best defined as a "structural contradiction," with attendant psychological feelings of guilt and uncertainty regarding the challenge of "blackness" that exists before them.

In addition to the Black Power period's signalling a rapid shift away from integration as a goal for those in the forefront of black political activity, the era also demanded, with equal swiftness, the replacement of a preoccupation with "whiteness" by a priority concern with "blackness." The need to come to terms with "blackness" by way of self- and group-identification became a crucial concern. The act of denouncing the previously emulated white model created the need for a black model which could satisfy the same functions as did the white paradigm. As I understand the definitions given to this process among black college students, the act called for two things: a black model or ethos to be established, and the exorcism of that which had already been absorbed from the white standard.

It is quite apparent that these circumstances—exorcism and black model building—would have their greatest psychological impact on those people who had based their existence on the legitimacy of those white goals cherished in the pre-Black Power period. The black middle class has been most affected because it has been socialized into accepting white standards.[6] The problem is perhaps compacted for those black college students who are in the process of having their identity affirmed in the values of the white ideal.

The bridge of education that had been used to move blacks "upward" from their world of values to those of the white world had already been travelled by the established black middle class during a period when acquiring a formal education and its attendant white values was totally acceptable. But with the emergence of a Black Power period the established black middle class began to feel the guilt, conflict, and the general psychological discomfort (indeed, even now insults and derision continue to come from the more militant sectors of the black community) that issue from having its position and values defined as "non-black." The black college student of today, travelling that same academic bridge with his vision toward being an affirmed, card-carrying member in support of white ideals, is by virtue of his status as a college student now forced to stop abruptly and face the "blackness" that has been historically the object of escape. The realities of the Black Power period have demanded of him a face-to-face confrontation with the black audience, the need to develop an operational definition of "blackness," and a decision as to how he will cope with this operational definition in both his private and public life.

The student has come to feel that "blackness" is a quality located in the community and is not to be identified with the campus academic experience or those involved in it. Therefore, he often feels less than "black." The definition given to "blackness" by students suggests that it does not

6 A little over fifteen years ago E. Franklin Frazier had this to say about the black middle class:

In escaping into a world of make-believe, middle class Negroes have rejected both identification with the Negro and his traditional culture. Through delusions of wealth and power they have sought identification with the white America which continues to reject them. But these delusions leave them frustrated because they are unable to escape from the emptiness and futility of their existence. —*Black Bourgeoisie* (London: Collier-Macmillan, 1969), p. 195.

mean being a structural "house Nigger" (which they see approximating their roles); it means being a "street Nigger"—out in the community fighting for it—not residing in the isolated towers of the university, studying about the street life.

How does the black college student respond to these charges of not being "black"? How does he demonstrate his "blackness" and yet maintain the status that generates the charges? The remainder of this chapter will devote itself to the analysis of these questions.

Black Student Unions

In the wake of the Black Power period a great number of all-black organizations emerged reflecting the sense of black unity and strength that is explicit in the slogan. These organizations have become notably visible in areas of social, political, and professional life that heretofore have been solidly committed to the ideal of integration. Black caucuses, or groups with other names reflecting the presence of an organized unit of black people, are to be found in the disciplines of the social sciences, in teacher organizations, in police associations, and in established political arrangements. The creation of black organizations not only indicates that the interests promoted by the original bodies are frequently at odds with those represented by the black units within them, but also reflects a newly found pride in being black and in letting others know it. The emphasis on playing roles that were recognized as "white" has now been replaced by an emphasis on roles that are recognized as "black."

Colleges and universities have witnessed the eruption of similar organizations. Black student unions, Afro-American associations, Soul student unions—all reflect the growing unity among black students on college campuses. These units have come into being as a response to the demands and ideology of Black Power.

Black student organizations have the potential for satisfying those aspects of black student life that frequently cannot be met by the traditional activities of the white campus community, usually because these activities are defined by black students as "white" and are in fact geared to meet the interests of white students. Activities such as rowing, hockey, chess, golf, and tennis are frequently defined as "white" activities by black students. Defining the activities as "white" keeps most black students from participating in them—whether there is interest in the activities or not. Other activities such as skiing or flying are considered not only as "white-oriented" by the black students, but are also seen as being prohibitive because of the expense involved. Participation by black students in any of these activities exposes them to charges of "being white" or "acting white." Rather than risk opening themselves to these charges, most black students prefer to go along with those affairs either sponsored by black organizations (various social affairs, dances, whist parties, etc.) or having the sanction of blacks (traditional activities such as football, basketball, baseball, and track).

Socially, black student unions have the potential for providing an atmosphere that allows black students to come together, to meet one another, and to share ideas and experiences before, during, and after the time needed for the student to adjust to his new environment. Academically, the organizations can provide students with an opportunity to discuss any number of issues germane to the concerns confronting the black community. The problem of day-care centers is one example. Students have drawn up questionnaires to assess the need, functions, and projected effectiveness of day-care centers in particular neighborhoods. Having done this, they have put together proposals requesting resources to operate. Analyses of the experience with the problems have focused on such questions as: (1) What contributions were made to the community? (2) What was learned about the community? and (3) What can be done to maximize success next time? The give-and-take in such activities helps the student satisfy requirements of general academic work while providing a broader understanding of the world he lives in.

Politically, the student organizations can foster a black consciousness among a number of students. This is important for enhancing the status of black people on campus, for making education a more relevant undertaking for themselves and other students, and for encouraging more students to involve themselves in projects undertaken in the black community.

It is difficult to measure the strength of a black student union on a college campus. Its presence indicates, however, that it is addressing certain needs of some black students, and that it is attempting to cope with policies and practices of the campus community which are at odds with the interests of black students. Many student organizations, for example, have been concerned with significantly increasing the number of black faculty and black administrators who are aware of the problems and aspirations of black students. The organizations have also been concerned with increasing the number of courses focusing on the black experience. Establishing black student organizations, then, is a prerequisite to correcting the inequities on white campuses that are noticed by the black students. Experience has taught black students that the only way to get "the man" to move is through constantly applying pressure. While it may be difficult to measure the efficacy of black student organizations, their presence has at least served to remind others that there are needs yet unmet within the campus community.

The intransigence of whites in colleges and universities is a primary ingredient found wherever there has been black student unrest. As V. O. Key, Jr., suggests, "To carve out a place for itself in the politico-social order [including the academic order], a new group may have to fight for reorientation of many of the values of the old order."[7] The struggle of the black student organization has been to "blacken the university." This contest recognizes three important factors. (1) The number of black students attending

7 *Politics, Parties and Pressure Groups* (New York: Thomas Y. Crowell, 1964), p. 57.

[34]

predominantly white universities suggests a systematic exclusion of blacks from higher education.[8] Statistics further suggest that the number of students is insufficient to meet the educational needs of the black community. (2) The absence of representative numbers of black faculty in predominantly white institutions suggests historical and structural intransigence toward black concerns. (3) The cultural experience of the black community has been largely ignored in university curricula. Frequently when this cultural experience has been included, it has been subjected to tremendous distortion. To carve out a place for blacks in the academic order requires that considerable attention be paid to the factors above. The efforts of a concerned black student organization to this end are encouraged and commended.

The need for a black student organization does not, however, *ipso facto* issue inevitably into a strong, viable organization commanding the respect and the allegiance of its black constituency. If it is true that the *need* for such organizations is beyond questioning, then it is imperative to examine those things that diminish their effectiveness. Consider, for example, these internal agents which psychologically undermine the viability of black groups, discussed by Alvin F. Poussaint and Linda R. McLean in an article entitled "Black Roadblocks to Black Unity":[9]

1. a distrust of and lack of confidence in black leadership;
2. the lingering image of all-black organizations as inferior;

[8] The most recent available information indicates that over eight million people attend college. Of this figure 680,000 are black with approximately 500,000 attending predominantly white colleges and universities, and the remainder in a handful of black colleges and universities. Based on blacks comprising 20% of the population, one would expect approximately 1.5 million blacks on white campuses, or three times the present figure. It is difficult to avoid the racial implications of this disparity.

Source for data: United States Bureau of the Census, "Enrollment Status of the Population (3-34 years old) by Age, Race and Selected Educational Characteristics," October, 1971, *Current Population Reports* (Washington, D. C.: Government Printing Office, March 1972).

[9] *Negro Digest*, XVII (November 1968), 11.

3. the cathartic and domineering attitudes of members of the organization;
4. the relationship between black leaders and white women, which fragments the group and discredits leadership;
5. the tremendous status needs of members of the organization, which undercut its smooth operation; and
6. the severe negativism of certain group members.[10]

Similarly, there are external elements which are harmful to the goal of achieving group unity:

1. the lack of financial support by blacks outside the organizations;
2. the difficulty in defining problems and setting realistic goals; and
3. the concentration on terminology and name-calling.

We caution the reader to keep in mind the above factors in evaluating the overall effectiveness of black student organizations.

Blacker Than Thou

In their article, Poussaint and McLean focus on problems they feel are endemic to black organizations. In connection with this concern, the authors also introduce the "blacker-than-thou" attitude with its gaming, competitive dimension. Their incisive discussion of this latter issue lends itself admirably to treatment in this work.

As Poussaint and McLean indicate, it is amazing and commendable, given all the internal and external problems cited above, that black organizations are able to function at all. The validity of the authors' application of these problems to black organizations in general is apparent to anyone

---

10 *Ibid.* In Poussaint and McLean's discussion, this factor is designated as an "external" factor. However, for the purposes of this study its significance is reflected more by its designation as an "internal" factor.

who has even been peripherally involved in these organizations. However, it is only when the authors discuss the problem of goal definition (number two under "external factors") and the related problem of "setting limits"[11] that they begin to focus on the specific concept which relates directly to the world of the black college student. According to their interpretation, the inability to "set limits" helps us understand a behavioral pattern that surfaces as black students attempt to adjust to the conditions that have abruptly redefined their value premise from "white" to "black." Poussaint and McLean explain:

> . . . members very often stand up to testify to their dedication and acceptability as black militants. They will display militant credentials and try to "out-black" each other. They may harangue against "honkies," proclaim what they are going to do and "put down" other people as being "Uncle Toms" and "handkerchief heads." *In essence, they assume a "blacker than thou" attitude*[12] (emphasis mine).

A typical expression of the problem of "setting limits" might go like this:

> The scene is a small auditorium on a predominantly white campus. It is filled with black students who are present to discuss an impending campus strike. The stage is occupied by several leaders of the campus' black student organization. The leaders have just stated that no black student under any circumstances will attend classes. There is considerable uneasiness about this decree among some students in the audience. State-

---

[11] In their reference to this problem, what the authors suggest is that if goals were clearly established, it would be easier for group members to determine the acceptability of other members. As an example of this point, they cite the following hypothetical situation:
   . . . if the purpose of the group was to solicit money, it would not be harmful for members to have white persons as friends. In fact, this could be advantageous. However, to take an extreme example: if the purpose of the group was to arm itself for armed combat against whites, it would be unrealistic to expect a black person married to a white person to participate; therefore, criteria could be more easily and less arbitrarily established.

[12] *Ibid.,* p. 63.

[37]

ments just audible enough to be heard reflect some of the sentiment about the decision: "Shee-it, I know they don't mean me, I'm too close to graduating"; and "Them muthafukas is crazy. I done spent all this money and they expect me to be doin' that shit?"

One of the students in the audience stands to raise some questions about the validity of the idea in light of the reason for which students come to college. One of the leaders retorts: "Nigga, you must not be "black" if you can't sacrifice something for the community. The community is sacrificing its ass every day for you." In the auditorium there is a silence born of intimidation. The student sits down, having nothing more to say, while the uneasiness still exists. No more students raise questions regarding the decision.

Scenes of this type are quite familiar to black college students. The scene suggests problems of "setting limits" by the leadership, but it also captures the inability of the audience (followers and/or constituents) to demand that limits be set for fear of having their "blackness" challenged by the leadership.

Poussaint and McLean see, in addition to the problem of "setting limits," two other elements contributing to the emergence of the blacker-than-thou attitude and its behavioral components: "the need to speak up and to release rage," and "their [blacks'] lack of an agenda and a program."

It should be noted that Poussaint and McLean discuss the genesis of the blacker-than-thou attitude peripherally and at times incidentally. If I have attached more magnitude to the genesis of this attitude than is suggested by the authors, I have done so because of its principal contribution to the thesis of this work. The gaming and competitive manifestations the authors cite, suggesting the presence of a blacker-than-thou attitude, are consistent with the observations and evidence I have gathered. However, the conditions the authors see as promoting the attitude appear to be at fault regarding their order in a cause-effect relationship.

Two of the factors seen by Poussaint and McLean, the "inability to set limits" and the "need to speak up and

[38]

release rage," have historically been associated with the black experience in this country. The "inability to set limits" was as characteristic of groups in the Civil Rights era as it is characteristic of groups in the Black Power period. There is similar historical significance in the "need to speak up and to release rage." The oppression embracing the total black experience in this country has always dictated the need to speak up—to release rage; but because of new circumstances and definitions, what is probably different now is the *content* of what is to be spoken rather than the *need* to speak. If there is any further difference it is in the form that the rage takes.

The third factor cited by Poussaint and McLean as contributing to the blacker-than-thou attitude is the "lack of an agenda and a program." The program of the Civil Rights era was better defined than that of the Black Power period. Its program was clear-cut in its quest for integration through nonviolent means. The program priorities of the Black Power period have yet to be established with the same specificity and singularity of purpose. Since there was a program and agenda prior to the emergence of the blacker-than-thou attitude, however, it is spurious to suggest that the absence of an agenda and program gave rise to the attitude.

It appears, then, that there is no causal relationship between the blacker-than-thou attitude and the factors cited by Poussaint and McLean. These factors are not new in the black experience in this country; but I suggest that they take on a renewed significance because of the new context (the Black Power period as opposed to the Civil Rights era) in which they are being considered. New definitions in political movements frequently call for different programs and different rhetoric. The new definition may also give vent to a new kind of feeling or rage to be released (blacker-than-thou). I offer that the Poussaint-McLean argument can be strengthened and more light can be thrown on the entire issue by expanding their framework to include the above thoughts.

A closer examination of the blacker-than-thou attitude in the political world of the black college student can now be considered. It is almost common-sense to expect that with the shift in orientation from "white" to "black," roles once governed, guided, and dictated by white norms would now be guided by the emergence of black norms, or by the recognition of existing black norms. The substance of these norms is to be found in the members of the black lower class and is built around the theme of "Who is the baddest?" and "Who"—by virtue of his affiliation with the style of life of the lower class—"is the blackest?" The concern here, as Poussaint and McLean believe, is to be able to "out-black" someone, to present more impressive militant credentials than someone else. To be able to do this places one in a self-appointed position of superiority. He assumes that his position legitimates his calling another black an "Uncle Tom," an "agent provocateur," a "bourgeois opportunist," or a host of other names designed to accuse someone of not being black." The precarious status of the accused, who has to answer to the degree of his blackness, using the accuser in many cases as the frame of reference, requires complicity. This shared but unspoken agreement allows the accused to respond directly to the accuser, indicating to him by his actions or his rhetoric that (1) the accuser is correct, (2) the accused is as black as the accuser, or (3) the accused is blacker than the accuser.

While some students actively pursue or adopt a blacker-than-thou stance, eliciting responses of the kind mentioned above, other students actively and conscientiously "demonstrate their blackness"; i.e., they dress, speak, and act according to the dictates of the total black norm, whether they accept and understand the norms or not. While many students play this role solely to avoid the charge of not being "black" enough, others are more serious in their intent to demonstrate that they are "black" and that they do identify with the black community.

The frequency with which individuals engage in any of the variations of the blacker-than-thou game does not fall evenly across the black student population. As we have pointed out, the blacker-than-thou atmosphere is a by-product of the Black Power Movement and of the black

[40]

student's resulting efforts to shift his allegiance away from the values of the white audience to those of the black audience. It is basically sustained by three types of students: (1) those who use blacker-than-thou as an instrument for their own self-aggrandizement, (2) those who use blacker-than-thou as an instrument to raise political consciousness, and (3) those who use blacker-than-thou to compensate for their feelings of insecurity regarding their blackness." Let us now consider in reverse order the social types conforming to these categories and their involvement in the blacker-than-thou atmosphere.

Black students who have been raised in a typical middle-class milieu, steeped in its values, and have escaped poverty, hunger, and other problems confronting the lower classes, have more difficulties than others in adjusting to the "new" values. For them, blacker-than-thou can be a source of compensation, as the following students demonstrate.

R28 is a twenty-six-year-old female graduate student. The combined salaries of her parents exceed $20,000 per year:[13]

> You know, because I haven't had to confront the kinds of problems that most blacks have faced, like problems of economics and housing and all that, I have often felt very guilty; and people try to make me feel less black because my experiences have been different from those blacks in the ghetto. When I first became aware of the blackness thing I was kinda shaky and I was afraid to mingle with the black community around here because of the emphasis on being black and blacker-than-thou and all that stuff, but often having been around the blacker-than-thou's—who do not impress me—I'm not overly concerned about being black enough. . . . But before I got to this point in my thinking I tried to be as black as I thought others were. I started cursing and I tried to be more like most black women are: brisk, harsh, have bad disposition—being nasty—and argumentative and headstrong. I was already headstrong and argumentative so I didn't have to work on that.

---

[13] See Appendix, p. 119, for a profile of the respondents interviewed for this study.

R17 is a twenty-one-year-old male senior. He is one of two children. His mother is a housewife; his father earns in excess of $20,000 per year:

I was kind of shaky about blacks when I first came here and nobody really helped me out—shaky about grooving with blacks, you might say; getting together and just talking to them; approaching them or anything like that. So when I actually tried to do certain things it was really hard. A lot of people didn't react like you might think people in a struggle or who had common bonds would react. If you say certain things that you have feelings about, people would say "you're not ready" or "you're a Tom." If your statements aren't a certain way you are stereotyped as not being black. Plus, if you don't have a certain background, like coming from a poor neighborhood or having certain experiences or being able to relate to certain things, you are made to feel different, like you did something wrong. I guess because my hair was straight and I was light-skinned didn't help much either.

R20 is a twenty-two-year-old senior. The combined salaries of her parents exceed $20,000 per year:

Because I don't come from the ghetto or a black neighborhood, I've felt for a long time that I've been missing something. I haven't felt as black as people coming from this background, so I've had to overcompensate. When I first came here I had to readjust to a totally new thing: middle-class blacks cloaking themselves in a different class; everybody acting like they're lower class. I found myself trying to take on those values. I tried to act like them; imitate them rather than be myself whether they accepted me or not.

Black students tend to assume that those blacks who have had more exposure or who have been more economically privileged have totally white values. There's no validity in this at all. Because a black from this background, even though he overcompensates for his blackness, has a truer sense of what's happening because he knows what "materialism" is all about.

R20 suggests the direction frequently taken by many from a middle-class background when he indicates that there is a tendency to "overcompensate" for one's black-

[42]

ness; i.e., many in their attempts to demonstrate their blackness become "blacker" than the audience they seek to emulate or identify with. These attempts issue into manifestations of blacker-than-thou or, at least, "I'm as black as you."

We must add that students from middle-class backgrounds certainly do not have a monopoly on the problem of adjusting to the definitions dictated by the extreme displays of black-orientation. The problem potentially exists for those of other backgrounds as well. Even for the student who is more certain about his "blackness" because of maturity and/or background and experiences, there is still the need for him to adjust to the demands required of the new situation of black college life. Yet, the issue of his "blackness" may not be one that he is preoccupied with. His attitude may be similar to that of R32 (a twenty-year-old junior, whose parents earn $9,000 in combined salaries):

> Baby, I know I'm black and I don't even want to deal with that shit; and I don't feel guilty for being here. Like after coming from Mississippi, Chicago, and Gary and not having any money and living in low income areas, I developed a philosophy of self-preservation. So when I got to school, man, I was elated. I said "man, this is out-of-sight"; like I finally got here. And when I got here those so-called militant cats were saying, "yeah, you muthafuckas, you shouldn't be up here going to school. You should be in the community." Now man, these cats were students too, telling *me* that shit. Yeah, I said, groovy; I been out there and I know in fact that the people in the community who are going through all them changes wish they weren't there. So, don't tell me I should be there going through those changes, when if I'm here and righteously doing my job here I can go back and deal with the situation.

There may be certain students, like R32, whose feelings of conflict or problems of adjustment have been minimal. We would argue, however, that the force of the black movement has been such that every black student has had to, at one time, question his "blackness" and what it means relative to his role as a student.

[43]

There are a great many students on campus who have both lived in a lower-class black community (ghetto) and tasted the bitterness of life that frequently characterizes its existence without partaking in its values and life styles. The parents of those making it to universities from these settings have dreams for their youngsters and, perhaps more important, some means, meager though they frequently are. They also have the ability to guide the interests of their youngsters along paths not unlike those of the middle class. And though these students may now boast of having been brought up in the streets and are familiar with many of the characteristics of street life, this experience has been gained from afar—without personal involvement. It is not surprising, then, to find many of these students suffering from the same problems as those from the typical middle-class environment. They, too, have had minimal participation in the realities of black street life. They also have occasion to question the degree of their "blackness."

Thus, the element of "class," *per se* (in terms of economic criteria), tells us only the degree to which individuals have or have not satisfied experiential "blackness" as defined by the prevailing norms. Physical markings of what are traditionally viewed as indicators of middle classness (and therefore, "whiteness"), such as straight hair, keen facial features, and light skin, often become conditions for indictments of not being black, whether one's experience complies with those charges or not. Whether a student is from a middle-class background or is believed by others to come from one, he feels some pressure to demonstrate his blackness.

The second category of students that contributes to the perpetuation of an active blacker-than-thou atmosphere is the black politicos. The black politicos are found in the leadership positions of the black student organizations. They determine the direction the organization takes, the issues that it deals with, and the ideology that guides the organization, frequently without the input of those who compose the "membership" and without the "following" of the organization. It is often a tightly knit cadre of a handful

[44]

of students who have gotten to know each other fairly well through social activities as well as political discussions who constitute the leadership.

While many of these politicos have been active to some extent in aspects of the Civil Rights Movement, their distinguishing characteristic is that they consider themselves full-time watchdogs for the black community, and that they have *the* answer for what the black community ought to be doing and the direction it should take. Those taking a different stance on these issues are regarded as "not knowing what's happening" and not being "black" enough to understand what should be done.

Since many of the black politicos regard themselves as *the* revolutionaries or militants on campus, they feel they carry the lion's share of the responsibility for politicizing the remainder of the black student population. Not only must they politicize the black student population through verbal and demonstrative expression of their militance and blackness; they also have the burden of demonstrating to their counterparts on other campuses and to the revolutionary brothers in the streets that they are worthy of being called "revolutionaries" and "militants" in spite of the fact that they are students—or maybe *because* they are students.

For those who attend well-known, predominantly white institutions, politicizing the black students and establishing a militant reputation become awesome tasks, and they have predictable consequences (as we shall consider in the next chapter). The "revolutionary" brothers in the street have the weight of self-appointed superiority on their side. These brothers are the standard against which the black politicos assess themselves. In this drama the black politicos stand in the same relationship vis-à-vis the black students on campus. Politically, the black politicos are sharper, more aware, and in many ways more sensitive to the plight of black people in white America than other black college students.

These factors feed the astute black politicos' feelings of guilt for being on campus, arousing their frustration for not being able to politicize as effectively as they wish. Meanwhile, their unbending attitude about what black people

[45]

should be doing frequently alienates those of other political persuasions—a situation often ending in exchanges of "You ain't 'black' enough" and "Man, you think you got a monopoly on the black experience."

R29, a twenty-three-year-old senior, has been actively involved in black politics on campus. He speaks here about the organization he was involved with and its relationship to the rest of the black students:

> The Afros (short for Afro-American Students Union) should have disbanded a long time ago because black students don't really want a black student organization. It was like they didn't want one and the organization was a thorn in their side trying to get them to do things they didn't want to do.
>
> The Afros has never done anything concrete to benefit a whole lot of people nor have the students here ever supported a black organization. Since black students don't seem to be ready to work together, the organization merely added to the divisiveness.
>
> The people in the organization have tended to be too political; whereas most of the students were socially inclined. The leaders of the Afros saw the world much differently than students on campus and it was impossible to resolve the two views. The Afros should have been more service-oriented, and provided a social arena. This way it would have spoken to students' needs rather than trying to mold them into the kinds of things the leaders wanted.

R27 is a twenty-two-year-old senior. He, too, has been active in black politics and closely identified with the leadership of the Afro-American Students Union. He recognizes the existence of the blacker-than-thou atmosphere of the politicos and its impact on others:

> One thing the movement has done is to produce people who engage in blacker-than-thou games. These people spend all their time worrying about the race—a full-time warning system for the black community which is a function that is needed. They occasionally take themselves too seriously. They don't see themselves as part of a whole. They see themselves as the only people who have some solution to the program and everybody who

[46]

does not agree is not as together as I am or is not as black as I am. This is to be expected because the black thing is so new. It has caused a lot of problems, but eventually these people will become fewer and fewer as they move into other areas.

The third category of student is the "blackness pimp." He differs from the students of the first type in that he feels more secure about his "blackness." He differs from the politicos in that he is less politically aware and has less political knowledge. He also has less interest and concern about the collective problems of black people as a whole than do the politicos. However, the "blackness pimp" is aware of the political utility of using "blackness" to advance his own personal situation. He, in fact, "pimps" the movement. Blackness is to him a commodity that has the value of a wild card in a poker game; he uses it in order to strengthen his own hand. In the classroom he will badger a black professor to give him an "A" solely because the professor is black, or he will denounce writing papers or taking exams as a "white" thing (therefore, the professor who may assign such tasks is not "black"). The pimp's primary concern is: "How can I use this blackness game to maneuver through the white man's system?" He is not so much a product of the movement as he is one who is apart from it, yet able to manipulate aspects of it for personal gain.

Much of the pimp's rhetoric cannot be distinguished from that of the politicos. Both assert themselves as spokesmen for the black community, and both announce their actions in the name of benefiting the black community and strengthening black unity (postures which are difficult for other students to challenge without risking the charge of being against black unity and therefore "non-black"); but they make their efforts for different reasons. The politico is honestly, though self-righteously, concerned about black people. The pimp is concerned about making it as an individual, although this is sometimes camouflaged by the banner of blackness that he waves.

While "blackness pimps" are also occasionally counted

[47]

among the politicos, their forte is in one-to-one relationships in areas separate from politics; here they use political
force and power for their own purposes, whether it is to get
a better grade, to maneuver an evening with a woman (black
or white), or to justify not taking an examination. They
know that black people don't like to have their "blackness"
questioned and that white people don't like to be called
racist. As long as the pimp has a target for his ends, he will
continue to manipulate. Thus "blackness pimp," along with
the middle-class type and the politico, provides the force for
the campus blacker-than-thou atmosphere.

There is nothing absolutely discrete about the three social
types presented here. There are degrees of overlapping
among the social types. This is probably seen most readily
between the middle-class type and the politicos. It is not
uncommon, for example, for students who previously were
strongly middle-class-oriented to be seen now in the leadership ranks of the politicos. Indeed, I would suggest that
nearly all black students have at some time reflected perspectives shared by one or more of these social types. For
some of the students, however, one of the social types has
become the point of emphasis around which his behavior
and his problems are organized and around which others
define him.

There is a much larger category into which most black
college students fall. Basically, they are committed to enjoy-
ing college life as it is without involvement in political
efforts by black students. While they wear bubas, natural
hair styles, and other insignias of blackness, it is usually a
defensive act to keep others from questioning their blackness while they pursue their education or their other concerns on campus. They are usually lumped under the category of "Uncle Toms" by those blacks active in politics. It
is the influence of these "Uncle Toms" on the identity of
campus blacks to which the other black students are opposed. In the eyes of the activist blacks, it is the "Uncle
Tom" who comes closest to meeting Malcolm X's depiction
of the "house Negro": ". . . they lived in the house with the
master, they dressed pretty good, they eat good. . . . They

loved the master more than the master loved himself. . . ."[14]

The blacker-than-thou atmosphere has profound consequences for individuals, and these consequences militate against the achieving of black consolidation.

I have suggested that middle-class values have been defined and looked upon by recent black norms as "white"— the white man's "thing." Since the black masses have been defined as lower class, it is here that we find the black man's "thing" and the essence of blackness. The slot allocated for the street brother, and such concepts as the "bad mutha," the "street Nigger," and "home boy" suggest the extent that black lower-class values have preempted middle-class values in the rhetoric of black college students. There is increasing difficulty in distinguishing the black college student from the brother in the street. Much of the similarity between the two is played out in exaggerated form on the campus.

On nearly every predominantly white campus there is a spot designated by blacks as their own. The spot is invariably referred to as "the wall," "the bench," "the rock," or, even, "the co'ner." The spot is normally strategically located near a main gate or entrance. The location allows for its participants to see "what's happ'nin' " and allows others to "check them (the brothers and sisters) out" (scrutinize them). Whites understand that it is *only* for blacks. Blacks not prepared to "be down" or "get down" (be black) are not welcome at "the co'ner." It is a place where the "real blacks" hang out (they are usually predominantly male).

A number of activities go on at "the wall" and usually at the same time. Some brothers may be "rapping heavy" about the revolution; others may be "rappin' " about parties, dope, chicks, or some other subject. Much of the "rapping" that goes on is "jive" (not serious), and is accepted as that by the participants. Indeed, one of the functions of "the wall" is to provide an outlet, a place

14 *Malcolm X Speaks,* ed. George Breitman, p. 11.

where one can relax and be with his own kind. It is also a place where a person does not have to deal with the white man. As one brother indicated to me, "It's a place where you can psychologically tell white people to get fucked, we don't need you."

Another function of "the place," as I see it, is that it allows its participants to proclaim to the rest of the campus its affinity with the black lower class. The mode of dress, the styles of expression, the boisterous humor, and the loud and frequent handslapping suggest considerable preoccupation with lower-class stereotypes. It is difficult to escape the impression that these and related activities are self-conscious articulations of identity with "blackness" and the oppressed ghetto masses. The norms of "the wall" are built on a celebration of values that in a prior period were denounced but have now become larger than life in their importance. This celebration is an effort by the students to refute their identification with the group-denying and self-negating hang-ups of an earlier generation.

The pressures of this new black norm have created, in combination with the blacker-than-thou atmosphere, a pseudo-culture on the campus that witnesses black college students reconstructing their past and their backgrounds to comply with its dictates. It is not unusual for a brother or a sister to deny his middle-class background and to relate to others that "I've always been a revolutionary," or "Yeah, man, I use to be on the streets evuh'day talking shit to the women and drinking wine," when both statements may be completely false.

R12, a twenty-one-year-old senior, feels that much of the reconstruction of one's past has to do with having been brought up to conform to the dictates of a norm that is now devalued. Here she speaks to this theory as it relates to men:

> Most of the brothers on campus suffer from a lot of insecurities about themselves as men. They discovered sex and women at a much later age than most black guys because most were sheltered in high school. While they were studying and making good marks so they could go to college, the other brothers were out in the streets taking care of business.

[50]

Now they (black college males) have developed a "bad complex." Everybody wants to be a "bad Nigger" and that indicates to me that they weren't bad when other people were bad. They watched "bad Niggers" as they were growing up, and now this is their chance to act bad. . . .

The reluctance to have one's blackness brought into question has created a need for some to assume blacker-than-thou dispositions, to act out street-Nigger roles and to reconstruct their pasts in ways conforming not only to the notion of being "black," but also to a creed of having always been "black."

Suspicion, distrust, and charges of people "fronting black" (pretending that one is black) permeate the world of the black college student. The weight of continuing to pay homage to the black norm without having a clear understanding of what the norm means or how to reconcile the norm to the role of being a student has provided the cause for two important phenomena: (1) a movement of blacks away from involvement in black student political organizations, and (2) the fragmentation of those blacks remaining politically active into more than one organization, each having its own definitive ideology of what "black" should be or is.

The effect of having one's blackness brought into question is a powerful force having profound and far-reaching entanglements for black student behavior. An examination of these complexities at a collective level—the strike at the Berkeley campus of the University of California—follows.

the struggle to "get it together": the strike at berkeley

III

On January 22, 1969, the Berkeley campus of the University of California—well known as an arena for radical student activities in addition to being well known for its high standing in the academic world—became the setting of fifty-two days of strike activities led by the Third World Liberation Front (a black-led coalition of the four major minority groups on campus—black, Chicano, Asian, and Native-American students).

The period of time between the beginning of the strike and March 14—the day a moratorium on the strike was called—was marked by picketing by the Third World Liberation Front and its supporters. Participants in the demonstration included students, administrative and faculty personnel, and many other people from campus environs and the community at large. On more than one occasion the number of participants in picketing activities exceeded a thousand. In response to the actual and alleged activities of the strikers, the Governor of California declared a "state of emergency," leading to the campus' being occupied by hundreds of state troopers, highway patrolmen, county sheriffs, policemen from surrounding communities, and local and campus police.

The fervor of strike activities incited polarizations. Few people were without strong feelings one way or the other regarding the merits of the strike *per se* or those secondary events that the strike generated, namely, the active presence of "peace officers" and the problems directly ensuing from their presence.

Charges and counter-charges characterized the relationship between the Third World Liberation Front and the administration. Similar attacks marked the relationship between the strikers and the police—a relationship that was heavily punctuated with beatings, arrests, and tear-gassing from the ground and the air. Some classes were cancelled and others were moved off campus because of the tenuous conditions created by the strike. Students soliciting funds for bail were numerous. First aid volunteers were stationed at strategic points on the campus. Volunteers wearing white arm bands were responsible for administering first aid to persons injured by tear gas or billy clubs.

From a handful of Third World Liberation Front picketers, the strike had grown in intensity to a point where thousands of students involved themselves, shouting, "On strike: Shut it down!," "Down with the Pigs." A veritable battleground between students and police ensued.

From a point of relative indifference to the demands of the Third World Liberation Front, the faculty moved to a position of supporting the movement's principal demand—a College of Ethnic Studies. Some of the faculty sympathized because they saw merit in the demand; others gave their support merely to stop the strike and return the campus to its "normal" functions.

Across the Bay at San Francisco State College, similar black-student-led activities were going on and had been going on for three months prior to the strike at Berkeley. So numerous were black-led militant activities across the nation at university and college campuses that many observers responded to the question, "Why the strike at Berkeley?," with "Well, it is just the year of the strike." Others indicted the University's slow recognition of the demands of the Afro-American Students Union as the cause. Yet others said, "They did it because San Francisco State did it." All of these responses contain a grain of truth.

Student Protests 1969,[1] a report published by the Urban Research Corporation, stated among its findings that there were 292 major student protests on 232 college and university campuses in the first six months of 1969, and that black students were involved in more than half of these protests. The fact that according to the findings the most frequent issue was black recognition, and that racially integrated protests were uncommon, is some indication of the extent to which black students either led or initiated such protests. So, while those who blandly attributed the Berkeley strike to its being "the year of the strike" may have been objectively correct about a phenomenon taking place across the country, such an answer does very little to tell us *why,* in fact, there was a strike at Berkeley.

Those who would place their emphasis on the reluctance of the University's administration to deal with black demands and on the facts surrounding strike activities at San Francisco State come much closer to understanding the actual circumstances that generated the strike at Berkeley. While it appears that the "year of the strike" and the "San Francisco State did it" arguments are the same argument—just a matter of moving from the general to the specific—the impact of the relationship between the black student populations at Berkeley and San Francisco is a crucial ingredient in understanding why the blacks at Berkeley struck. It is equally important to understand the extent to which the grounds for striking had been properly fertilized by the administration and by the traditions of university life. There are, then, numerous reasons why the Berkeley strike was called.

Why the Strike Was Called

The strike at Berkeley was a complicated political, social, and psychological maneuver that can only be explained by examining a variety of factors. For purposes of analysis it is important to separate the objective conditions that provided

[1] Urban Research Corporation, *Student Protests 1969.*

a context for the strike from the subjective interpretations of actors who called and sustained the strike. First, the objective conditions can be subdivided into two categories: (1) internal conditions on the Berkeley campus, particularly the conflict between the Afro-American Students Union and the University's administration over the issue of a Black Studies Department; (2) the existence of the strike at San Francisco State College and, to a lesser extent, strikes and militant activities taking place at other campuses throughout the country.

However, it is the subjective rejoinder to these conditions that is crucial for understanding the dynamics of the strike. How black students at Berkeley viewed themselves on the spectrum of "blackness" is also relevant.

Given the publicly stated reasons and the rhetoric that has in general accompanied the most militant activities of black students on campuses across the country, it is not surprising that one of the most popular explanations of the strike from black students related it to the existence of institutional racism. Added to this was the unwillingness of the University of California to correct part of this unjust reality by establishing a Black Studies Department along lines suggested by the Afro-American Students Union. The fact that the University of California operates and has traditionally operated on a singular standard of excellence based on values derived from a white European experience, and that its faculty, its administration, its student body, and its curriculum have always been overwhelmingly white, substantiates the charge that there has been a historical exclusion of nonwhite peoples and nonwhite perspectives. While these facts have always been blatantly clear, it is only with the appearance of the Black Power Movement that their significance has been dramatized as characteristic of a racist society.

In a sense the university is a microcosm of the American society at large and, according to a growing number of students and observers of the campus scene, it requires the same kinds of pressures and confrontations to change it that are viewed as necessary in the larger society. Indeed, this was the public reason given by the leadership for the Berkeley strike. The specific issues were the racism at the University, and the reluctance of the University in responding to the demand for a Black Studies Department to alleviate certain aspects of racism.

As accurate as this microcosm thesis may be, the demand for a Black Studies Department (which eventually became a demand for a Third World College as the strike activities got under way) was not, as I see it, the most compelling reason why the strike was called. Both the need and the desire for a Black Studies Department were real, and this demand was a factor contributing to the strike's being called and sustained; however, the most compelling reason for the strike was directly related to the fact that there was a strike going on at San Francisco State College. The platform of the leadership at San Francisco brought into question the "blackness" of the leadership of the black students at Berkeley. The production of an effective resistance tactic (work stoppage) for the ostensible purpose of acquiring a Black Studies Department was a convenient way to end all doubts on the questions of "blackness" at Berkeley.

Black Studies Department Argument

On April 4, 1968, Dr. Martin Luther King, Jr., was fatally wounded. The impact of his death was felt throughout the nation and especially in the black community. In some sectors of the community the feelings of anger were so great that many residents found expression for their distress through rioting. Dr. King's death may have been responsible for awakening black students to the need to do more than they had previously done to get the college community to respond to the black experience.

In mid-April, 1968, a small group of Berkeley's Afro-American Students Union met one evening to discuss what could be done to strengthen the presence of the black experience on Berkeley's campus and how to get other black students to understand what it meant to be black in white America.[2] After several hours of discussion it was decided that the group would develop a proposal for a Black Studies Department. Some time was spent arguing the pros and cons of having such a department on a white campus controlled by white interests. While most of those present recognized the advantages of having such an enterprise located in the black community and operating independent of white controls, they also realized that the location of funds would be an obstacle not easily surmounted. However, since black people pay taxes as well as whites, it was decided that the University belonged as much to blacks as to anybody else. Thus, it was decided that the department should be located on campus.

After several other meetings geared to what the character of a Black Studies Department should be, a proposal was written and submitted to the Chancellor and his staff for consideration. By late summer the Chancellor appointed a black Associate Professor in Social Welfare to the position of Assistant Chancellor for Academic Affairs. One of his functions was to implement this proposal for a Black Studies Department.

While the Assistant Chancellor for Academic Affairs was involved in meeting with various committees and individuals regarding the expeditious establishment of a Black Studies Department, monies were allocated to establish five courses in the fall of 1968 that focused on certain aspects of the black experience. These courses, however, were to be housed in existing departments.

Strategically, the five-course program was an expedient arrangement while the administration and faculty deliberated the merits of the proposal submitted by the Afro-American Students Union. The black professor and influential members of the Afro-American Students Union found themselves being increasingly excluded from such deliberations. Even a second document, amplifying the students' proposal and submitted by the Assistant Chancellor, received little defense by its authors. As a consequence of

2 The author was among those present.

[57]

examination by various University committees, a proposal was drawn that cut out two features of the initial proposal: (a) students would have a strong voice in setting up the department and operating it; and (b) a major thrust of the Black Studies Department would be community-oriented. The charges of omission which radically altered the entire focus of the proposed department were made public in an article by Third World faculty and administrators in the campus newspaper, *Daily Californian,*[3] which cited factors that led to the strike:

> ... In December and January, Dean Knight's Executive Committee of the College of Letters and Science reviewed the proposal for a D.A.A.S. (Department of Afro-American Studies). Assistant Chancellor Billingsley and the black students who had worked on the proposal were not a party to these deliberations. (That would apparently have "compromised the integrity of the review procedure.") For only a short period of minutes Dr. Billingsley and the black students testified before the Committee.
>
> No blacks sit on the Executive Committee of the College. Thus, when other politically powerful voices from other politically powerful whites in the Academic Senate appeared to testify about Black Studies, white men were talking to white men about what was good for the blacks.
>
> It was at this critical juncture that forces were set in motion that led to the current crisis[the strike activities]. The black students heard through second- and third-hand sources that white men were decimating their original proposal, deleting the essential community-oriented features of that proposal, and turning it into a traditional academic-scholarly-classroom-stale approach to "The Negro."
>
> Adding fuel to this was a second and third hand report that only Harvard-type Negroes would be recruited to this new D.A.A.S., thereby assuring that the staff would be oriented to publication in professional journals, not to the immediate concerns of the nation's black ghettoes. ...

Pursuing this argument, the seeds for the strike were planted by the University officials in their unwillingness to

3 *Daily Californian* (February 21, 1969).

involve blacks in decision-making sessions regarding the destiny of the Department of Afro-American Studies. As a result, decisions made by the committees were at odds with that on which the black students had placed the most value: the community-oriented aspect of the proposal and the right for students to have a strong voice in determining what should go on within the department. These facts, coupled with the cumbersome, time-consuming, bureaucratic procedure that the Chancellor insisted upon, generated hostility and distrust.

Having shared their experiences with members of other minority groups that subsequently composed the Third World Liberation Front, the black students decided that no faith could be put in the white policy-making machinery of the University. What was called for was a strike to achieve an autonomous Third World College with each minority group having its own department. It was argued that a structure of this type would free each of the departments included in the Third World College from the "archaic, racist" traditions of the College of Letters and Science, where the Department of Afro-American Studies was to be established.

On the last two school days of the week of January 13, word began to circulate throughout the Third World campus community that there was going to be a strike. Since only a handful of those respected as the leadership of the Afro-American Students Union were knowledgeable about the problems of getting a Department of Afro-American Studies established, the news of a strike caught most by surprise. Yet hundreds turned out for meetings designed to discuss why the strike was being called. In a meeting on Friday, January 17, in an atmosphere filled with indictments against the administration for "shuffling their feet" on the request for a Black Studies Department and against the black students for not being concerned about the "community" and the goal of revolution, not one voice was raised in dissent when the question was raised, "Should we strike?" It was finally agreed that picket lines should be set up Wednesday, January 22, 1969.

The University officials' recalcitrance significantly contributed to the strike's being called, due to their failure to change their review process. Their ignorance of the need to maintain the integrity of black people as human beings and to seek ways of changing the conditions under which blacks live is a factor that cannot be minimized. Indeed, the frustration experienced by many black students in sitting through all-white classes, listening to white professors speak about and analyze problems of blacks from a white perspective, was enough to encourage many to involve themselves in the strike.

Although this theory of the University's responsibility for the conditions that gave rise to the strike at Berkeley is viable, it is not sufficient in and of itself to explain why the strike took place. Indeed, the contribution of the University was not even a necessary—although it was a contributing factor—for the strike to be called. One has to look for the precipitating causes of the strike in the relationship existing between the blacks at the University of California and the blacks at San Francisco State College. One must consider the meanings given to each by the other in the context of new black definitions and the consequences of these new concepts. And finally, one must examine the ties between Berkeley's black militants and the rest of Berkeley's black student population, ties arising from the relationship between the acknowledged militants of both campuses.

"Blacker-Than-Thou" Argument

The University of California at Berkeley has achieved international stature as one of the most prestigious of all institutions of higher learning. The black community sees the University as being designed for the "rich, white, and brilliant." Although the advent of programs at the University to increase the minority population has given hopes to blacks who do not fall into any of these categories, the image still remains intact. Accordingly, those blacks matriculating at the University are viewed as being "bourgy blacks"—blacks coming from privileged backgrounds, whose parents are doctors, lawyers, and teachers. Those whose backgrounds are not professionally and financially prestigious are expected, by virtue of the image and nature of the campus life, to be socialized into acting like "bourgy blacks."

On the other hand, San Francisco State College was viewed as a place for those blacks who "don't have what it takes" to go to the University of California. Thus, those blacks going to the University of California were seen as intellectually superior to those going to San Francisco State College. The fact that only a handful of blacks was ever known to study at and get degrees from the University of California, while hundreds of blacks have always studied at and graduated from San Francisco State College, reinforced this image of Berkeley.

These images of the two institutions made it convenient to describe the blacks at Berkeley as "house Niggers" and the blacks at San Francisco State College as "field Niggers." The advent of the Black Power era and the influence of the Marxian perspective of the Black Panther Party (and especially the influence of this organization on the Black Student Unions in the area) also contributed to the distinct dichotomy.

The uncomfortable position of blacks at Berkeley was compounded by their being on one of the nation's most radically active campuses. White radicals led the Free Speech Movement (FSM) of the early 1960's, a movement virtually free of participation by individual black students or black student organizations. This movement was defined as "white" and not warranting the involvement of blacks.

In the celebrated Eldridge Cleaver case at the Berkeley campus, again it was the white radicals who took the leadership in pushing the case. The black student organization excused its noninvolvement on the grounds that Cleaver had not come to the blacks first and, as a result, whites were taking the leadership and trying to determine the character of black involvement, a situation which the black student organization would not accept.

The Cleaver situation, however, differed substantively

[61]

from the FSM situation. The issue of racism was paramount. Here was a black man whose politics had made him one of the most controversial and exciting figures in the country, whose experiences had equipped him to be one of the most knowledgeable and insightful persons on the meaning of the black experience in white America, and whose publications defied any criticism of his intellectual capabilities. Yet he was denounced by the governing structure of the University of California as unfit to lecture on race relations! For many, including some outspoken professors on campus, it was a case of blatant racism; for others the refusal was a denial of academic freedom. There were many, including the Black Panther Party, who questioned the passive role of the Afro-American Students Union in this issue.

These two political events have been among the more popularized ones to have taken place at Berkeley not involving active participation of black students or black student organizations. The black students' image of noninvolvement, especially those who referred to themselves as "militants," reinforced a growing image of Berkeley's blacks as bourgeois. It was easy to excuse blacks from not participating actively in the Free Speech Movement, as the movement did not appear to relate substantially or even tangentially to the purposes of a black movement; there was, of course, the obvious exception that many white sympathizers of the black movement were involved in black activities, and for the purpose of "each scratching the other's back" support of some kind might have led to greater support for the black movement.

Then came the strike at San Francisco State College in November of 1968. It was sustained for five months before it was called off, making it the nation's longest and most publicized student strike of the 1968-69 school year. It had been in effect for three months before the blacks at the University of California decided to go on strike. The black militants at Berkeley were heavily chided and criticized by the black militants at San Francisco State for their inactivity, complacency, and lack of demonstrative support for the strike at San Francisco.

[62]

In light of this, black militants at Berkeley were finding it increasingly difficult to justify to themselves and others their self-designation as "militants." The rhetoric that had been employed to defend their inactivity in the celebrated FSM and Cleaver issue—"white radical things"—was seen as an excuse for a lack of "blackness." The pressure to strike and to engage in some kind of militant activity became unbearable for some of the leaders of Berkeley's black student organization. Black Studies, an issue that had engendered extreme emotionalism on a number of campuses in the country and was at the heart of the strike at San Francisco State, became the all-encompassing motif of the strike. *Anyone against Black Studies was obviously in favor of white studies and could not possibly be black.* This kind of thinking became the primary basis for the strike at Berkeley.

The Afro-American Students Union at Berkeley had difficulty in politically mobilizing the black students. Among a large segment of the black student body there was a growing lack of confidence in the Afros as a serious, well-meaning black student organization. The leadership knew that they could not announce that the strike was being called because "we want to prove our blackness." Such a position would not only reflect unfavorably upon the black students in general, but would also raise even more questions about how "black" a leadership is that makes a statement like this. The issue of Black Studies (later the Third World College) became the publicly announced reason for the strike. In essence, it was decided that a strike was to be called even before it was clear what the announced reasons would be; and although the leadership was reluctant to concede such a position during the strike, their tones during interviews indicated that their degree of "blackness" was the real issue.

R27, an active leader in the strike and a known leader of the Afro-American Students Union, explained the strike in the following manner:

> We wanted to prove to San Francisco State that we were as bad and as black as they were. It was a way of resolving the problems of guilt and conflict.

[63]

In the eyes of the leaders, the strike was conceivable one day and the next day it was the only thing left. It was not something decided upon by the masses of black students. It was pushed across. We had to prove that we were bad because the organization was accused as not being militant enough. . . . My decision to strike was an emotional decision rather than one of calm deliberation. It was done in an emotional black-power kind of manner.

R29, like R27 a recognized leader of the Afros and the strike, gave these reasons for the strike:

Most of the pressures were from outside essentially. There has been a rivalry between the black student organizations at San Francisco State and Cal ever since they first began: more so on state's side than Cal's, but it exists here, too. So, when San Francisco State went on strike the pressure kept mounting for Berkeley to do something. It would have been an extreme loss of face for Berkeley not to have gone on strike. That provided the atmosphere for the strike being called on campus more than the issues. I think that the issues could have been resolved without the strike.

Berkeley has the image of being bourgeois, and Berkeley's black militants have been trying to live that down for a long time. They tended to be very sensitive about that. I was surprised that Berkeley held off as long as it did; but there was that pressure from State and from other people for Berkeley to stand up and do something.

There was a significant part of the black leadership that was against the strike from its inception; thought it was ridiculous. There really was no need to call the strike. However, the leadership called the strike because there were some who felt under a lot of pressure to do so. Many of the black students felt a pressure to strike also. They wanted to strike just to take the pressure off and that was the only reason. They wanted to be able to say "Berkeley struck and I go to Berkeley." This took pressure off them.

The relationship between the general black student population at Cal and its leadership paralleled the relationship between Cal's black leadership and that of the San Francisco State strike and can be calculated, in general, on a

[64]

spectrum of "blackness." The Berkeley leadership saw the San Francisco leadership as being "blacker" than they, and their need to prove that they were as "black" as the latter was a moving force for their political behavior. Just as San Francisco State's black militants were able to maneuver Cal's into a strike position by questioning their "blackness," so the black leadership at Cal was able to pressure black students (and black faculty and administrators) to assume a similar position. While the blacker-than-thou attitude assumed by the black student leadership met with a certain degree of success in gaining black student participation in the strike, there were those who did not strike because of the intimidating aspects of the strategy. Similarly, there were those who thought the strike would have been more successful had there been less of this tactic.

R1 put it this way:

> If you want somebody to go on strike you don't start off by calling them bourgeoisie-ass niggers who ain't never did nothing, and don't know nothing about the community and this is your big chance, and if you don't we kickin' yo' ass.
>
> There was too much castigating and degrading of students and not enough persuasion and encouragement. I was surprised there was as much involvement as there was from black students.

The coercive designs that accompanied the imposed "blacker-than-thou" atmosphere on the strike created a situation of strain, hostility, and distrust between the leaders and the black strikers. However, there were students whose feelings approximated those expressed by R21, who states:

> I don't think the leadership influenced me either way as to whether I should strike or not. I listened to everything that was said and I came to my own conclusions as to why I was striking. I wasn't very impressed with what they were saying and if I were going to strike based on what they were saying I don't think I would have. I had sort of ignored the leaders and was striking for my own reasons. We should have a College of Ethnic

[65]

Studies, and because this is my school I felt like me and rest of the black students on this campus were important and we should be treated as though we are important. I really, really wanted Ethnic Studies because I want to learn about black people, too.

Others, for the most part, saw engaging in strike activities as a way of conforming to the demands implied by the concept of "black unity" and avoiding the indictment of not being "black" enough. This combination of fear and the idea of black unity created an atmosphere that made dissension from the decisions of the black leadership virtually impossible.

Those who were bold enough in black student meetings to question decisions or to take issue with certain aspects of the conduct of the strike were subjected to one of two maneuvers. Either they were shouted down by the leadership as "agent provocateurs," "spies," "pigs," or "counter-revolutionary bourgeoisie niggers," or they were invited to become part of the decision-making machinery. R36, a twenty-year-old sophomore, expresses feelings regarding the former certainty:

Like during the strike a lot of people used to make me sick because everybody wanted to accuse everybody else of being an agent. People would stand up in meetings and say so and so is an agent or point and say that person is an agent and this person is an agent. Everybody thought someone was an agent to blacker than anybody else, y' know. If I accuse someone of being an agent obviously that would make me feel blacker than him because he is more so a tool of the man than I am. People were always making these kinds of comments about people and they really didn't know whether the other person was an agent or not. Maybe they didn't like each other; or the person was strange or an outsider who had never participated in the Afros [Afro-American Students Union]. They figured he couldn't possibly be as black as they were because they were involved in the Afros [and he was not].

While such an atmosphere thwarted open criticism and open dissent, it did not thwart feelings of resentment

[66]

toward the leadership—feelings of being treated like "stupid, unthinking individuals being responded to in a contemptuous, high-handed fashion"—on the part of a significant number of strikers, including a large majority of those interviewed.

The Leadership

Sentiments regarding the effectiveness of the black leadership during the strike and their sincerity ranged widely. Some strikers were critical of the ability of the leaders to conduct the strike, but praised their sincerity; some praised both. Most, however, were critical of the leaders' effectiveness and their sincerity.

The black leadership of the strike was not a leadership chosen by the strikers but one that was imposed on them because it was carried over from the Afro-American Students Union, a black student organization on campus which met with marginal success, at best, in attracting students, mobilizing activities, and addressing issues. R12 was on campus when the organization first started and continued as a supporter. She states:

> The leadership of the strike was composed of those who had failed in the past to make the Afros a meaningful organization. The Afros from its inception has been a clique that has gone from one leader to the next leader—all involved in the same clique. In essence, this clique would determine among itself whose turn it was to be leader and meetings would be called to make it legal. . . . They were very self-protective of each other. They would never point out when someone was wrong. . . . I don't know if they were trying to protect some kind of friendship, trying to keep a woman from taking over the organization, or what. I see the same kinds of things happening in the strike. It is the same thing all over again.
>
> It seems that of nothing else but the combination of their errors they should come up with something better than what they're doing. I know there were a lot of times during the strike that people wanted to quit. They'd say "the leadership is jiving; they're full of shit. They always talking about somebody going

[67]

to get them on conspiracy charges." The leaders were afraid. They would say "you gotta protect your leadership; we can't do this, we can't do that cause the man is here and we'll all be up for conspiracy." They were so afraid of conspiracy. It seems to me they would abdicate their leadership because they didn't want the responsibility and the possible burdens of being singled out for punishment; but they wanted the power.

This negative image of the leadership was widely shared by the black strikers. Their behavior as a group during the strike reinforced those feelings already held by those familiar with the Afros; it also established disrespect on the part of those who had not known them before. There were a number of factors that contributed to this generally negative image: (1) the strike was called hastily; (2) there were tactics of intimidation and fear; (3) the conduct of the strike was chaotic. As one of the leaders, R27, stated, "In the eyes of the leaders, the strike was conceivable one day and the next day it was the only thing left." This fact caught the overwhelming majority of the black students on campus by complete surprise. Many did not hear about the strike until the day the picketing started. There was no real educating of the students regarding the issues, nor, as has been pointed out, was anyone but the leadership clique involved in making that hasty decision to strike. Perhaps more importantly, no groundwork for unity among black students had been established by the previous work of the Afro-American Students Union—a fact which probably had something to do with the supposed need for fear tactics and intimidation in getting black students to strike.

R23, who became one of the main "lieutenants" during the strike, largely because of his "muscle" (although he is also a very bright student), reflected on the strike in the following manner:

On this campus there is no real black consciousness or love between the brothers and the sisters. What you had regarding the strike was a small clique that decided to go on strike and make the rest of the students move because the clique felt it was time for a black movement to get active on campus. They

[68]

themselves never presented any ideas about how people can get together on this campus; how we should relate to each other or any thing like that. They simply forced the students to come out and walk picket lines; did not hold any large-scale political education courses; did not tell them they were doing this for the communities and not for themselves.

As a result, as the strike began to falter the students developed a strong resentment towards the strike. In fact, they called a number of the leaders "jive-ass dudes"; that it was a "jive strike"; a "jive thing." It wasn't worth it. If I had to do it all over again, I wouldn't do it. That's the wrong kind of attitude you're supposed to have coming out of a strike; and if the leadership had effectively done their job there would have been a different kind of attitude. It would have been the beginning of a movement as opposed to an end.

Tactics Employed to Get Blacks to Strike

Once the strike was decided upon by the leadership, the word was given to its handful of loyal followers. Leaflets flooded the campus announcing the strike and encouraging black students to attend meetings where discussions on the issues were to be held. The campus newspaper, the *Daily Californian,* and the grapevine also became vehicles of communicating the pending strike. After a brief discussion of the issues was presented, the day to begin the strike was confirmed. Even during this process the atmosphere was filled with intimidations and threats of bodily harm to those blacks who did not strike, who went to classes, or who came to work. These threats were in addition to the blacker-than-thou tactics.

A number of black students contributed to the strike by not coming to campus at all during the hours of normal strike activity (generally 8:00 a.m. to 4:00 p.m.). While some did this to honor the strike, others did it for fear of otherwise getting hurt by the black leadership or the musclemen. Similarly, many other students spent some time in the picket lines because of these fear tactics. There were some who took the position of R2:

[69]

I tried on several occasions to get clarification about demands of the strike from strike leaders, but all I ever got from them was hostility, threats, and intimidation. The fact that I asked them questions seemed to them as evidence of disloyalty to the cause. They were asking me who the fuck was I to ask questions. Because of all this hostility and threats I chose not to support the strike. In fact, I deliberately crossed the picket lines after I was threatened not to. I don't think a very small number of people should be telling others what they had to do.

The Conduct of the Strike

The black leadership of the strike composed one fourth of the group delegations that comprised the central committee, the policy body of the strike. The other delegations came from the three other minority groups that formed the Third World Liberation Front. This body decided what direction the strike would take, the general tactics employed, the nature of the negotiations with the administration, who would do what, and what would be said by whom to the press. Decisions made by this body flowed to designated "lieutenants" for implementation. This body met in total secrecy, moving around from place to place, alternating the meeting days and times to avoid being spotted by the police. On occasions a lieutenant, or one from each of the four minority groups, would be posted outside the meeting chambers as guards, watching and reporting anything that looked suspicious, and screening those who approached places where meetings were held. Non-members who were occasionally invited to attend central committee meetings were asked to be at a certain spot at a certain time to be escorted to the meeting.

The practice of having two, three, or even four bodyguards to accompany certain black leaders on and off campus for meetings was fashionable during the strike. It was also in vogue to have guards stand watch outside a place where a black leader was hiding (while he sent messages to those in charge of picket lines), or to have them do such things as buy lunch.

[70]

The rationale given by the leadership for having this aura of secrecy involved concern of their being assassinated or charged with conspiracy. The interpretation given by most of the strikers, however, reinforced their negative image of the leadership: "If our asses are out here on the [picket] line, theirs ought to be out here too."

R7, a female graduate student, offered some interesting insight on the techniques of the leaders:

> The strike was a replay of a poor movie. The leaders were doing all the little things that they heard people do in revolutions: put your leaders undercover, give out little secret messages, put people through FBI clearance before they can hold almost worthless positions, meet in secret. They had all the fixtures which are assigned to large-scale activities—which probably don't even operate there—and that was the only thing that seemed to have registered with them previous to the strike.
>
> The leadership was very paranoid, hiding out in rooms in the dorms rather than being on the picket lines.

R14, a male graduate student, expressed similar feelings:

> The leadership was using a revolutionary ideology within a bourgeois reformist framework; and when they did it was hypocritical. Like they would say "Yeah, man, let's take care of business, but if you get your pictures taken don't come back to campus; or don't get busted more than once." We found out that they did not do things they said they were going to do. There were a lot more chicken-shit muthafuckas than I thought.
>
> Another thing, the leadership was somewhat less than willing to undergo the burdens of leadership with respect to danger. Like the first week of the strike three so-called Afros were afraid to speak on the steps of Sproul Hall for fear of being shot. How chicken shit for them to think they were important enough for someone to waste a bullet on. I wouldn't waste shit on them.

While the black leadership, with the exception of a few, explained their virtual absence from the picket lines and their general noninvolvement in strike activities as in the

[71]

best interests of the strike (because it protected the leadership), the general feeling of the black strikers was that the leaders were abdicating very important aspects of their leadership roles, and this raised questions about their sincerity and their commitment to the strike.

Consistent with the expressions above are those made by R29, a leader of the Afros and of the strike. While he was against the strike, he joined because his friends were on strike. He states:

> The leadership got pretty Hollywood in terms of assessing their forces and the University's forces. Sometimes some of us would have to stop them and tell them "Hey, we don't have an army." A lot of times the leadership would be planning as if we had a cohesive, well-drilled army.
>
> The leadership did not have the students' welfare at heart. They provided an atmosphere where students took a lot of unnecessary risks. The leadership tended to get hung up in their own egos more than the welfare of the followers. As a matter-of-fact, it became almost like a chess game where the police were the pawns of the University and the students being pawns of the leadership. . . .

Strike Sustenance and Success

The ability to evaluate the strike at Berkeley presumes some knowledge of why the strike was called: why, in fact, people struck and what their goals were. In addition to the demand for a Black Studies Department (or Third World College) and the desire to answer San Francisco State's challenge of their "blackness," there were two other reasons for striking that were stated frequently: there were those who struck because of a commitment to the concept of black unity, and others who struck to reduce the tension of guilt arising from the need to prove their "blackness."

Strike success had different meanings for each of these groups of people. For the two latter groups emphasis was placed on the process of striking itself. This was also true with respect to those whose primary reason for striking was

[72]

in response to having their "blackness" and militancy questioned by the militants at San Francisco State College.

This latter group differed from the group that struck to reduce tension from guilt and frustration. For the tension-reducing group the strike was primarily cathartic. The external goals for which the strike may have been called were secondary to internal reasons for striking. While the cathartic aspects of the strike also applied to those responding to symbols of "blacker-than-thou-ness," for this group the task of the strike was twofold: (1) asserting and affirming "blackness" as a private individual concern, and (2) fulfilling the same concerns on the more public level to satisfy San Francisco State. For this group, too, the establishment of a Black Studies Department was of secondary interest—yet crucial to sustaining strike interest. It was the vehicle through which their primary reasons for striking could be satisfied.

For those whose primary reason for striking related to the concept of black unity, again the establishment of a Black Studies Department was of secondary interest. The primary interest for them (and their conditions for determining strike success) related to the issue of whether or not black people could work together. Whether the "man" had them all put in jail or all kicked out of school did not matter. The announced goals of the strike were issues subordinate to the goal of sticking together, no matter what happened.

For those striking primarily for a Black Studies Department (and Third World College), strike success had to do with whether or not such would be established as a result of the strike. To this group striking was one of several options that might be employed to get a department; the means was basically a secondary issue.

As stated earlier, the dominant influence on the direction and character of the strike came from those responding to the blacker-than-thou challenge. The combination of the strategy directed toward satisfying this goal and the strategy directed toward the goal of a Black Studies Department (or Third World College) had the effect of giving a schizophrenic character to the strike. The leadership had announced

[73]

that the goal of the strike was to achieve a Black Studies Department; meanwhile they pursued a strategy that was geared to proving they were "as black and as bad" as San Francisco State College. The question for them was, Could the strike create as much havoc as the one at San Francisco State? Could the extended struggle last as long? Could Berkeley attract as much attention? As many troops? As much gassing? To have gotten a Black Studies Department without having the campus become the focus of the national press would not have satisfied them. Indeed, there was ample evidence to demonstrate that a Black Studies Department could have been achieved without the strike's taking place. The concessions from the administration accompanying the moratorium on the strike were glaringly similar to what was offered prior to and at early points during the strike.

Thus, a response to the question "Was the strike successful?" is contingent upon which of these goals was the primary basis for one's participation. For those persons whose primary purpose was alleviating or minimizing tensions stemming from guilt or frustration, the *act* of striking and participating in strike activities was sufficient. They were able to take a stance and to make a gesture against racism. For this group the strike was a success, for it provided a tension-reducing activity. The degree of its success for any individual in this group was determined by the intensity of his involvement in the strike.

Both R17 and R38 typify the sentiments of this group. R17 says:

> I participated in the strike because I wanted to demonstrate my blackness. I wanted to prove that even though I am middle class I could get involved in unmiddle-class activities. Once I got involved it was important that I stay involved. To me it wasn't a part-time thing. I wanted to show that I was as bad as the next cat.

R38 expresses the same feelings:

[74]

I struck because I was an activist and I would have done anything that was proposed at the time. I was just growing politically and I wanted to see black people do something together. To a great extent my striking was like saying "I'm as black as the next person." Wanting to get involved is really wanting to demonstrate one's blackness. Wanting to be accepted by blacks here and wanting to show the brothers on the streets that the University is not messing up your head even though it is, had a lot to do with my striking.

Although both of these students expressed some negative feelings about the strike's success in terms of black unity, the strike was seen as successful for them in terms of its tension-reducing functions.

For those students whose primary interest was in giving some concrete meaning to the concept of black unity, the strike was not generally thought to be successful. While the act of the strike itself and the presence of black students on picket lines was an important manifestation of black unity, the conduct of the strike created more resistance toward the idea of "togetherness" once the strike was ended than was the case prior to the strike. A significant number of black students felt alienated from affecting the direction and character of the strike, and, more important, these students had great feelings of resentment toward the leadership. For a sizable number, black unity was the glue that prevented them from terminating their participation in the strike or publicly denouncing the leadership.

The delayed anger and disgust felt during the strike was expressed when the strike was over and took form in a lack of interest in reestablishing a black student organization. At least three meetings were called to elect new officers for the Afro-American Students Union. In addition to there being no more than twenty-five students at each of these meetings (of approximately one thousand black students, according to the Educational Opportunity Program office on campus), no one would allow his name to be placed in nomination for any office. This was a reflection both of the level of general disrepute that the Afro-American Students Union had fallen to and also of concern about the danger surrounding the head that wears the crown.[4]

While there were questions prior to the strike as to the meaningfulness of the Afro-American Students Union, the conduct of the strike removed any lingering doubt. Also the strike created among the black students such an atmosphere of hostility and distrust that suggestions about establishing a new organization were not greeted with enthusiasm, nor were they viewed as a serious proposition.

R5 was one of the more vehement spokesmen for the "black unity" people. She states her feelings on what was happening during the strike:

> Whether the strike was a good idea or not was not important. We would have been the winners if we could have been united and stood together. We couldn't do it.
>
> They [black students] didn't know that deep down all that mattered was that we stood together. If the strike was a crazy idea, so what? All we needed to show was that if anything came down—no matter how stupid—all that mattered was that we stand up there together and united. They couldn't do that. They were so wrapped up in themselves. Niggers took mo' back roads to this campus than in any time in history; even went through mo' back doors than they did during slavery. Niggers was scurrying around here getting to classes. They didn't care enough to see that all that mattered was that we stood together; but nobody wanted to jeopardize what they had—which wasn't shit anyway. They ain't got nothing. They dream of being a black physician and all that shit. That ain't gonna work. If your people don't move, you don't move. If the white man can stand up and call me a nigger, he can call anyone a nigger!

R24, although less vehement, focused his feeling in the same direction:

> I struck because even though I thought the leaders were making a mess there ought to be unity, and I thought I should

4 Prior to the termination of the strike, arguments over which black organization would have the most influence over the Black Studies program at the University of California at Los Angeles led to two black students' being shot and killed.

be a part of it. The strike, though, alienated a lot of people from the possibility of future struggles around issues that might be very important. I don't know if I would ever become involved in another situation like this one, and I say that because I wouldn't want to get involved in another situation where I put my future on the line behind a lot of bullshit like I did during the strike. It really ended up being a lot of worthless bullshit. The only good thing that came out of the strike is that I got to know a lot of people. It wasn't a good experience at all.

So my reasons for striking had more to do with the concept of black unity and togetherness than it did the issue of Black Studies, even though that was a good issue, too.

Black students striking for a Black Studies Department appeared much more critical of the strike than those falling into other categories. Because they concluded that there had been no need for a strike—that a Black Studies Department could have been gotten without a strike—they focused on the damage that the strike did to the concept of black unity and to individuals who were arrested, beat up, who flunked out of school as a consequence of engaging in strike activities. They also registered their own personal resentment of having engaged in the strike.

R31 puts it this way:

> I don't think the strike was successful. The only thing that happened was that people got their heads busted and thrown in jail or kicked out of school.

R23 agrees:

> The strike was not successful. The types of things that we got the administration was prepared to give anyway. So, I don't think we got anything out of the strike except for a lot of hostile feelings by a lot of black people towards one another.

Thus, the severest criticism of the strike came from those striking principally in the name of black unity and those striking for the establishment of a Black Studies Department.

For the remaining category of strikers—including the

[77]

leadership of the strike—the character of the strike took the shape of vindicating Berkeley's blacks against the indictment of not being "black." It was not in the interests of the leadership for the strike to be terminated after a short period of time even if a Black Studies Department had been established. The conditions that would have satisfied and expedited the establishment of a Black Studies Department would not satisfy the need to demonstrate that Berkeley was as "black" as San Francisco State. It was only when it became obvious (toward the beginning of finals in the Spring Quarter) that only a handful of blacks would continue to give a substantial or even minimal part of their time to the strike that a moratorium was called. Even then it was emphasized by the leadership that the strike was not over and that it was merely being placed in abeyance.

According to those who shared the goals of the leaders, the strike was successful. Even though it didn't last as long as the one at San Francisco State, or gain the same amount of public attention, the stoppage did satisfy the attending variables of duration, publicity, troop numbers, etc., and it stifled any legitimate criticism about Cal's students not being as "black" as anyone else—especially as "black" as those at San Francisco State College.

Another dynamic of the strike deserves mention here. The nationwide notoriety and publicity of the strike (and of course, its duration) resulted more from decisions made by the administration in consultation with the Governor and county and local law enforcement agencies than from the deliberate strategy of decision-makers of the strike. Were it not for the presence of hundreds of law enforcement agents called to campus during the third week, chances are the strike would have ceased after that time. Certainly it would never have reached the proportions it did at the height of its activities.

Until the third week, it was evident that Third World students were having difficulty (especially blacks) in involving members of their own constituencies and in appealing to white radicals and white student organizations for their involvement. The advent of hundreds of police on campus met with the disapproval of the white radicals and even of many students who were normally indifferent to political activities on campus. The strike gained momentum and its ranks were filled by thousands of students—nearly all white—who were not attracted to participation in the strike prior to the coming of the police. In essence, the strike turned into an anti-police demonstration.

Thus, the involvement of whites in the strike activity was largely based on anti-police feelings and not pro-ethnic-studies feelings. For them the success of the strike was related to its being an anti-police demonstration. Their involvement enhanced the public attention drawn to the strike and further led to decisions by the administration on the campus and the Governor of California which escalated the intensity of the conflict.

A Final Note on the Strike

Apart from the purposes black students had for engaging in strike activities, the strike had certain results that are important in their own right, in terms of politicizing the black students.

The strike was an exercise in political education. For many black students this was their first experience of involvement in an activity with political overtones—and especially in one basically organized and run by blacks. This experience produced an atmosphere on campus that many had only read about or experienced from a distance. Issues, problems, and rhetoric that had been dealt with in the classroom or in isolated meetings of black students (coming together for a variety of purposes—mostly social) were placed in the context of a real life situation. For many black students found themselves in a situation where they became objects of concern for the police and the courts—they were handcuffed, arrested, jailed. This experience allowed the students to declare a removal of the experiential obstacles that separated them from their black brothers and sisters in the streets. They became, as they saw it, part of the black community and its historical struggle for survival.

[79]

Their actions (they surmised) proved to the brothers in the street that the same conditions that characterize the larger society are also present within the confines of the university, and that similar action is needed to confront and eliminate it. Feelings, ideas, and beliefs became clearer and more crystallized in one way or another. As a consequence of their participation in the strike, many were able to deal more clearly and candidly with themselves as black individuals who shared privileges not offered or available to the black masses. R11, a twenty-year-old sophomore, expressed his feelings about the strike in the following way:

> I got more out of participating in the strike than I've gotten out of my last sixteen years of life. It was painful; it was beautiful; it was ugly. I think I lived more in those eight weeks than I have for a long time. My life moved awfully fast. It really did. I had to become more aware of what I was capable of doing and not doing, so as to know if someone confronted me with something and if it was something I knew I couldn't do there was no reason to feel guilty about it. I became aware of my assets and limitations. Until you can define your own limitations as far as the Black Movement is concerned you are going to feel guilt about the things that other people are doing that you aren't doing.

The strike also dramatized the University of California as being—along with other institutions in this society—in need of radical changes to keep abreast of the rapidly changing social conditions that are characterizing this society. It demonstrated that their past failures, traditions, and history must face up to the present realities and the challenges made upon them today if they are to remain (or become) viable and relevant to the entire human context surrounding them.

black man, black woman: "them changes"[1]   IV

The concept of "blackness" carries with it the potential for black unity, i.e., the ability of black people to celebrate the history of their common culture and struggle. In the black experience, however, certain barriers erected by whites—barriers of class, complexion, age, and sex—have depreciated the power of organized ethnicity—the one thing that other ethnic groups have found essential in negotiating their way to power positions in this country. Carmichael and Hamilton support this contention:

> *Before a group can enter the open society, it must first close ranks.* By this we mean that group solidarity is necessary before a group can operate effectively from a bargaining position of strength in a pluralistic society. Traditionally, each new ethnic group in this society has found the route to a social and political viability through the organization of its own institutions with which to represent its needs within the larger society. Studies in voting behavior specifically, and political behavior generally, have made it clear that politically the American pot has not

---

1 "Them changes" refers to "going thru changes," and is a phrase popularly used to characterize the fluctuations of black conjugal and romantic life. These troubles in the black community are most evident, and these kinds of experiences most exquisitely expressed, in the blues ethic. For an interesting analysis of the blues and its relationship to the black community in this respect, read Charles Keil, *Urban Blues* (Chicago: University of Chicago Press, 1966), especially the chapter "Role and Response."

[81]

melted. Italians vote for Rubino over O'Brien; Irish for Murphy over Goldberg, etc. The phenomena may seem distasteful to some, but it has been and remains today a central fact of the American political system.[2]

One of the most pervasive and destructive themes in the black community, caused by the vicious modality of slavery and racism in this country, is an invidious drama that casts black men and black women as adversaries to each other. The negative effects of such a drama for black unity are quite evident.

My intention is to explore the historical sustaining of one particular pattern of black male-female relationships. Specifically, I will examine some of the many facets of black male-female agitation on an integrated campus, the effect the turmoil has on black male and female students' views of themselves and each other, and the implications of the problem for the Black Student Movement.

Primarily, I will consider two dominant historical strains that have produced this drama. One emanates from the influence of slavery on the black family. The second develops from the American preoccupation with whiteness. It is this preference for whiteness that allows for a portrayal of the white woman as the "goddess of the Universe," and for a one-sided (white) definition of "woman-ness." This definition is worthy of consideration if attention is to be focused on black man-woman troubles. An examination of these two strains, then, takes us to the core of those circumstances that militate against, or impede the generation of, black unity on the predominantly white campus.

There is no need to belabor a discussion of the wretched, destructive consequences of the institution of slavery on the black family. Much of that history is now common knowledge. It is important, however, to understand that the seeds for much of today's discord between the sexes were planted and nurtured in the era of slavery. Ironically, the same sordid conditions creating the social image of the black man

2 Stokely Carmichael and Charles V. Hamilton, *Black Power,* p. 44.

as a stud and an irresponsible liability for his woman were also at work making the black woman self-reliant and self-sufficient. An equally important correlate was the effect of the slavery experience in developing in each sex an attitude toward the other that was increasingly consistent with their respective social images. Unfortunately, the opportunities for an emerging sense of black manhood were undermined by the conditions imposing an undesirable independence on the black woman. Even emancipation did very little in the ensuing years to effect any significant reversal in either the images of the black sexes or the conditions of slavery that generated them. Frazier seems to indicate this when he says:

> As a rule, the Negro woman as wife or mother was the mistress of her cabin, and, save for the interference of master or overseer, her wishes in regard to mating and family matters were paramount. Neither economic necessity nor tradition has instilled in her the spirit of subordination to masculine authority. *Emancipation only tended to confirm in many cases the spirit of self-sufficiency which slavery had taught*[3] (emphasis mine).

Interestingly, Price Cobbs and William Grier, two black psychologists, suggest that the culture of slavery was never undone, and that continued racism conspired to sustain the black man's image of being "irresponsible," "shiftless," and "lazy," and good only for satisfying bedroom desires and increasing the black population.[4]

The respective images of the black male and black female have survived from generation to generation. The survival of these images in the black community is seen frequently apart from the realities originating and perpetuating them; i.e., the images are seen as qualities of those affected, rather than properties of the system. Thus, it is not unusual for a black man, even when he has a meaningful job, to view his woman as a potential "castrator" and to be constantly on his guard against that possibility. Nor is it unusual for the

[3] E. Franklin Frazier, *The Negro Family in the United States* (Chicago: University of Chicago Press, 1939), p. 102.

[4] Price M. Cobbs and William H. Grier, *Black Rage* (New York: Bantam Books, 1969), p. 20.

[83]

woman, even if her man is working, to continue working or somehow seek ways of maintaining an aura of self-sufficiency, for fear that she cannot totally rely on her man. Basically, then, the effects of the racism and slavery that originally caused these problems still exist in American society.

The legacy of slavery, then, as it informs the historical black man-black woman relationship, provides an important backdrop against which much of the current perplexity between black men and black women on predominantly white campuses can be understood. Further, the problem is enlarged because of the demands of the Black Power Movement. These demands explicitly advise that the black man should assert his manhood and that the black woman should be submissive and dependent upon him. Important though this legacy of slavery may be, perhaps the second strain, the "mythical goddess of the universe," is more evident and direct in its omen for black unity on these campuses.

The Mystique of the White Woman

A major factor contributing to the trauma between the black male and female is the tremendous idolization of the white woman and the taboos surrounding her image. The deification of white women is a special mark of the general primacy given to the concept of "whiteness" in this society. "Whiteness" has been equated by the American culture with purity, good, freedom, beauty, and other valuable qualities. Consequently, the white woman has been displayed as the most concrete and tangible manifestation of all these qualities and virtues. Black women, on the other hand, have through a racist argument become walking repositories of the opposite of all the virtuous attributes of white women.

White women have been defined as the exclusive domain of the white man. Laws and codes of ethics were established to keep it as such. The white man's obsessive fear that black men are obsessed with desire to have sexual relations with white women has at times been so strong that punishment by lynching, castration, and electrocution has been meted

[84]

out to black men for merely looking at or—as the Emmitt Till case demonstrated—whistling at white women.[5]

While history has placed the white woman on a pedestal, Calvin C. Hernton states:

> The Negro woman through the years has suffered (and endured) every sexual outrage (with all of the psychological ramifications) that a "democratic" society can possibly inflict upon a human being. The sexual atrocities that have been done to her personality as a female creature, is a tale more bloody and brutal than most of us can imagine. I believe it was a black woman who first uttered the words: "Nobody knows the trouble I've seen."[6]

As a sexual object the black woman was historically a commodity for both black and white men; with the former she was a breeder of more slaves, and with the latter she was a testing ground where young whites came into manhood, or a sexual toy for those who had already become fully grown.

Hernton argues that historically the white woman has been sexually attracted to black men, and that it is she who is the aggressor and not the black male.[7] He also argues that the taboos surrounding her, the deification of her as "the ubiquitous sex symbol of our times," and the laws and mores denying the black man access to her have generated within the black man a "sociosexually induced predisposition for white women." Essentially, Hernton thinks that the black man has fallen victim to the myth of the sanctity of "white womanhood." In his chapter "The Negro Male," he concludes:

> The white world is virtuous, holy, chaste. The black world is dirty, savage, sinful. At the center of the clean world stands the

5 In August, 1955, Emmitt Till, a 14-year-old black from Chicago, was visiting his grandmother in Mississippi. For treating a white woman to his Southside wolf whistle, he was kidnapped, shot, and dumped in the Tallahatchie River.

6 *Sex and Racism in America* (New York: Grove Press, 1965), p. 123.

7 *Ibid.,* p. 21.

white woman. To Negroes who feel and suffer the atrocities of racism and inhumanity with intensity, one of the necessary components for transcending or "cleansing" the sin of blackness from their beings is to possess a white woman. According to the myth of white supremacy, it is the white woman who is the "Immaculate Conception" of our civilization. Her body is a holy sacrament, her possession is a sort of ontological affirmation of the black man's being. . . .[8]

Eldridge Cleaver, the noted black militant and author, exaggerates the direction that some black male-white female relationships take through his character, "the Accused":

There is no love left between a black man and a black woman. Take me, for instance. I love white women and hate black women. It's just in me so deep that I don't even try to get it out of me anymore. I'd jump over ten nigger bitches just to get to one white woman. Ain't no such thing as an ugly white woman. A white woman is beautiful even if she's baldheaded and only has one tooth. . . . It's not just the fact that she's a woman that I love; I love her skin, her soft, smooth, white skin. I like to just lick her white skin as if sweet fresh honey flows from her pores, and just to touch her long, soft, silky hair. There's a softness about a white woman, something delicate and soft inside her. But a nigger bitch seems to be full of steel, granite—hard and resisting, not soft and submissive like a white woman. Ain't nothing more beautiful than a white woman's hair being blown by the wind. The white woman is more than a symbol to me. . . . She's like a goddess, a symbol. My love for her is religious and beyond fulfillment. I worship her. I love a white woman's dirty drawers.[9]

The extent that white women and black women are equated respectively with good and evil is voiced by "the Accused" when he says:

Every time I embrace a black woman I'm embracing slavery, and when I put my arms around a white woman, well, I'm hugging freedom.[10]

8 *Ibid.,* p. 25.
9 Eldridge Cleaver, *Soul on Ice* (New York: Dell, 1968), p. 159.
10 *Ibid.,* p. 160.

Thus, the legacy of slavery and the myth of the sanctity of "white womanhood" work together to create problems between the black sexes, and to pose obstacles that thwart the ability of black college students to comply with the Black Power mandate of unity.

While the legacy of slavery and the myth of the sanctity of "white womanhood" concur in causing the battle of the black sexes, the proximity and availability of white women on the campus give the white woman variable more explanatory power among black college students. Indeed, it appears that the "white woman variable" has taken on an unprecedented dimension in informing this problem.

As I interpret the situation of the larger black community—as opposed to the student community—Grier, Cobbs, Cleaver, and Hernton have given unwarranted elevation to the place of the white woman in the desires and yearnings of the black man. I would contend that the overriding time- and energy-consuming task of survival in the general black community has dwarfed and continues to dwarf any preoccupation with "sleeping white." Conceding for a moment the existence of psychological yearnings for white skin on a level suggested by the above writers, the sociological manifestations of such yearnings are further thwarted by the caste-like nature of race relations. Thus, in the larger society the combination of survival and caste-like race relations reduces the issue of "sleeping white" to insignificant proportions. A battle of the sexes remains in the larger black community, nurtured by the residual effects of slavery.

It is only within the province of the integrated campus community, in very recent years and against the backdrop of exhortations to black unity, that the issue of the white woman in black male-female relationships takes on the significance indicated in both the interviews and in the works of the authors quoted here—a situation that is apparently created as much by the interests of white women in black men as by the males' interests in them.[11] My conclu-

11 I do not mean to suggest in this discussion that the white-woman issue is a new obstacle for black unity even in social movements. There has always been

[87]

sions on the problem of student unity among the sexes are drawn heavily from the black students themselves, both male and female.

R14 is a thirty-year-old, male graduate student:

> Black females are more hostile to black males than they have ever been. A lot of people rationalize and say it's got something to do with white women, but that's bullshit. It's partly due to that, but that's not totally it because it seems to me that . . . well, I think it's a copout. I don't know why there's so much hostility.
>
> There's something hypocritical about having to force yourself to relate to sisters instead of naturally relating. The whole notion of like seeing a brother watch a fine white girl go by and say to themselves "damn, she sure is looking good." Like I see them saying it, but then they will go force themselves to go over and rap to a sister when they don't think the same thing, don't feel the same way. There's something very hypocritical about that kind of situation.
>
> Brothers and sisters don't seem to be able to deal; the reason is we black men are beginning to feel our oats, you know, like the Man has let us kick him in the ass a few times, loud talk him a little bit; now we're going to get his thing which we've been wanting for a long time anyhow—the white woman. The black man has more freedom. White women are beginning to dig us and they have been the standards for a long time which has really been drugged into our heads. Unless a woman looks white in terms of having those features we really don't dig her that much.
>
> Black women are still very middle class in their orientation. Like you can't go up to one and say "hey baby, what's happening?" because half the time they don't speak and from what I can see if they say "hello" they feel they got to give you their pants. To give you that much, like a hello, is to give all. So they don't say shit to you.

---

a down-played discussion by civil rights workers of the problems engendered within the movement because of intimacies between black men and white women. While the integrationist ideology gave the intimacy a certain protection, the emotional feelings of many black women were not consistent with such an ideology. The problem of black men and black women is all the more important now, because the Black Power ideology suggests it should not even be an issue—yet it is a central sore point.

R32 is a twenty-year-old junior:

Man, the brothers and the sisters don't get along too well. The cats say it is hard to relate to sisters because the sister does not understand that a man needs sex, and she doesn't want to get off of it. She puts you through a whole set of changes. . . . Being on this campus is like a foreign thing for us. We are removed from our natural habitat and there are added pressures that keep us apart. Like for the black man, there is a whole new array of available females and, like myself being a man, I'm ready to swoop on anything that is swoopable. This type of philosophy doesn't go hand in hand with the sisters' philosophy.

I know a lot of cats hustling and playing a sex game with white women; making themselves sexually available to attain shelter, food, and clothing. A lot of cats doing this have previously gone with sisters and they had a very bad relationship. Since the white chick will give them more loving and care without any arguments than would a black chick, the brother is more tender and warm towards her.

The black movement has made both the brother and the sister stop and evaluate what's happening. Hopefully, it will bring about some unison in blackness between the two. Blackness is a vehicle by which we both can travel the gulf which is between us, and get together. So far it is not coming about. . . .

But even if she had the material goods she'd be afraid to give it to the man because she's afraid of being exploited by him. Man, like I've been called all kinds of dogs. She is very suspicious of the intention and purposes of the black man, and that suspicion drives both to the point where they are reluctant to give of themselves to make the relationship work.

The traditional behavior of the black man towards his black woman justifies her behavior. He has been disrespectful of her. From childhood the sisters have been taught "you better watch out; those black cats will swoop and be gone and you'll be left holding the bag."

R26 is a twenty-one-year-old sophomore:

The relationship between the brothers and the sisters is not one of harmony. The black female is intellectually superior. We [black men] haven't had the chance to get ourselves together intellectually because we've been too busy trying to get that masculinity thing defined in ourselves.

[89]

On this campus we have a funny kind of woman. We have what is called the black American college woman, and she is superior to the average college black man. The black man has a lot of work to do to catch up. This creates conflict because we can't tell them anything because they think they know everything—which they really do. So most of the chicks want cats intellectually compatible with her and most of the cats feel below her and this creates problems.

The movement is trying to get more respect for the black male. . . . The movement has been designed to give the black man a chance to be a man, to dominate the black woman. Most of the chicks on this campus prefer to dominate you. The movement is designed to give the man his penis back and I don't know if the black woman is ready for that. She can accept him in the traditional role, but this new black image frightens her, I think.

The black woman feels insecure because of the black man digging on the white chick. They call the black man "jive time dudes" if they express a desire to sleep with or be with white women. The black cats rationalize by saying they're doing it for money or for other reasons. The black woman really doesn't know how to combat this, but she tells him he is not black if he doesn't deal with her.

R38 is a nineteen-year-old sophomore:

On this campus in particular what prevents a harmonious relationship is the fact that a whole lot of black dudes dig on white chicks and the sisters resent it very much. It may be a majority of dudes doing this because I see a hell of a lot of cats with white women. This frustrates the sisters very much.

The brothers go with white women number one because she is the Western standard of beauty; number two is that black men are irresponsible. They've been made irresponsible by the nature of this society because they've had no opportunity to be responsible, and because of this they don't like to be tied down by anything. When a black dude meets a sister he usually has to show a whole lot before he can take her to bed. He usually has to make some kind of commitment to her before he can have that full relationship. A brother can pick up a white woman and do what he wants, split, come back a couple of weeks later and pick her up again because it is just a sexual attraction that they

[90]

both enjoy without committing himself. So, the brother is saying to the sister, "Black woman you can't do too much for me right now. I need a broad to whom I don't have to make any commitments; I need a broad who can give me some bread."

A lot of black dudes feel they can express themselves better to a white woman than they can to a sister. They feel they can be more honest to a white woman about how they feel about things. Many of the brothers have a stereotype about the sisters being hard, too rowdy, too cold. So they prefer the white women. Black women try to compete with white women too much. They try to be superfeminine. They want to be looked at like white women. They want to have pretty legs and wear short dresses like white women, and have the make-up on their eyes like white women. I don't think it's too cool, but unfortunately a lot of black women are jealous of the white women, especially those who can't pull too many dudes. There are some sisters just being themselves saying "Here I am Brother. If you want me, come and get me. I ain't putting on no wigs and make-up for you, but I am mellow."

The feelings expressed in the foregoing statements typify those of the male respondents in the survey. They feel that their relationship with black women is not good, and that it is now worse than it has ever been. Whether or not this is true is probably less important than the belief that it is so. The question to be raised is, "Why is it that in an atmosphere that calls for black unity and the celebration of blackness such tension exists between black men and women on a college campus?"

The answer to this question is found in the new set of definitions from the Black Power Movement and, based on these definitions, the expectations of a different behavior. From the belief that "black is beautiful" and that black unity is essential, it should follow that past problems of black male-female relations would be eliminated—or at least significantly diminished—as black people moved closer together in their politics and their thinking. While there is evidence that black people are coming together, the rhetoric has preceded the action in such a way that deviations from the goals make all the more bitter the very problem that

[91]

rhetoric alone seeks to diminish—i.e., the notion of the superiority of whiteness and the inferiority of blackness. It becomes increasingly apparent that while rhetoric has utility as a direction-giver, only action can provide the substance; and even with action, the assumption cannot be made that action reflects commitment, for this is not automatically the case.

From the black male point of view, the black movement has special precepts for him. He defines the movement as being designed to give him the opportunity to assert his masculinity against an oppressive white world and against the black woman. This situation becomes complicated for him because of the availability of white women as sex mates, with an ease and in a supply not existing with the black women. Further, the stereotyped image of the black woman as a "castrator," as "hard, loud, and rowdy," continues to be operative, and she is therefore seen as a barrier to the full affirmation of black masculinity. The white woman becomes to the black man a path of least resistance. Not only is she more free with her physical gifts, but she is also viewed as much softer and more understanding—traits viewed by the black man as highly compatible with his coming to grips with his felt masculine needs.

The price he pays for "talking black" and "sleeping white" is the wrath of the black woman and pangs of inner guilt and conflict. He feels that he has deviated from the norms demanded by the black movement. For some black males the attempt to alleviate this guilt leads only to the increased anger of the black woman. That is, the gravity of the black norm encourages a spurious relationship in which the black man feels compelled to posture a romantic involvement with a black woman for whom he has no feeling or commitment. The black woman is not respected for who she is; instead she becomes an object allowing the black man to fulfil his obligation to the black norm. R14, above, suggests this question of hypocrisy when black men feel forced to relate to black women, whether they wish to or not. Another informant, R19, is more succinct on the issue of the black woman as an object:

[92]

People try to force me to live my life the way they live theirs, and I get a feelin' when I'm around a lot of people who talk that cultural stuff that somehow it seems hypocritical to me. Like all of a sudden man, cats are saying you have to be with a black woman, and the question that I raise is whether you're going with that black woman because it is the fashionable thing to do or do you respect her as a woman; doing it because it is the thing to do is exploiting the chick.

The problem of seeing the black woman as an object in the sense suggested by R19 seems to reflect, unfortunately, the visual limitations of some black men. The theme of sex is recurrent throughout the statements made by the black college males. If, as R26 says, the black movement is "designed to give the black man back his penis," it appears also that he is thoroughly interested in using it. The white woman will let him, while the black woman will not without sending him through all kinds of "changes" he feels he should not have to go through, because of the availability of white women and especially because of the relationship among blacks that should exist according to the theme of black unity. However, R32's statement suggests that some men's sexual appetite knows no politics or ideology:

Like for the black man, there is a whole new array of available females [on campus] and, like myself being a man, I'm ready to swoop on anything that is swoopable. This type of philosophy doesn't go hand in hand with the sisters' philosophy.

By implication, R32 offers that it is too bad that black sisters would place the sexual appetite of black men in an ideological context; he feels that the issue of masculinity should not be viewed from a black nationhood perspective. Finally, R38 implies a certain positive "specialness" for black women. In the second paragraph of his statement he indicates that black men are presently going through a lot of changes which require some sexual experimentation without commitment. For this purpose white women are quite suitable. He implies that when it is time to make a commitment the brothers will seek out the sisters.

[93]

Notwithstanding the hints of a disguised optimism in R38's statement or R32's indications of a misunderstanding of what black men are doing and why, the black woman does not occupy the centrally important role among my informants that I would expect. The black woman in this drama is first seen as the symbol of the matriarch—hard, cold, dominating, and demanding, and therefore the traditional emasculator of black manhood. On the other hand, she is viewed as the epitome of the middle-class ideal, complete with puritanical sex values. As such, her behavior does not lend itself to cooperating with the black man's definition of manhood and his understanding of the black movement. So, in either case the black woman is surveyed by the black male as an obstacle to the establishment of black manhood.

The Black Female Student Perspective

R28 is a twenty-six-year-old graduate student:

> Black woman are upset because black men are running around with white women. That's really a big problem that a number of black chicks have.
>
> Black women feel very insecure about this thing. Black men always talk about black women so harshly. You know, like they say black women never know when to keep their mouths shut; they're dominating and castrating and all that. The black men do this without regard to the history of what has happened to both of us in this country and without really seeing that we're pitted against one another.
>
> I have my personal problems with black men because I have a real problem with men who are uptight about being castrated and who are always talking about it and all that, and always putting black women in those kinds of bags. My personal attitude is if you're a man, be a man and you don't have to worry about the rest of it. I guess I should be more openminded and helpful, but I'm negative about it and I really don't want to hear it.
>
> It's going to take a while before "black is beautiful" is believed, but I think eventually it will be. The black man goes

with white women because they still believe that whiteness is still the standard of beauty, and that "black is beautiful" is only a slogan.

R10 is a twenty-one-year-old senior:

Black men are hung up on white females and that is having its effects on the campus black movement because it is driving women away from participating. Black women feel there is hypocrisy and a double standard when black men rap "blackness" in meetings and then strut around on campus with blondes on their arms.

I also feel that black females on campus are not carrying themselves in a way to achieve proper response from black men. They have adopted too many caricatures from white society. Too many black women want bread-winners and somebody they can show at the socials. They want a very compassionate butler who is good with children. Black women appear more bound by white values in this area than whites themselves. Black women are in a more defensive position than white women and demand "super-respect" from black men because their womanhood has been trampled over. Black men are not patient enough for this.

What black men are doing is bad politically speaking. The movement requires black men and black women getting together. The problem is that it is more than just black men making it with white women. It is also the contemptuous "shut-up-sit-down" attitude that black men have towards black women. The reason for this attitude when it exists is that, just in asking people I've noticed that black guys who had a lot of regard for their mothers, mothers they really respected and really loved, have a much more positive attitude toward black women generally, whatever their other experiences have been, than those who have the sort of screaming, matriarch type of mothers. I think this is sort of what the black guy feels he is overcoming when he tells a sister in a meeting to sit down. It is sort of a deep-rooted type of problem that isn't just a question of the availability of white women.

R13 is a twenty-year-old junior:

As long as a black doesn't seek a white partner because of something lacking in the black opposite, and black being nega-

[95]

tive, it is O.K. with me if they're together. But most of the black guys say they go with white girls because they cannot deal with black girls. They do not have to prove themselves to white women. Black women expect more in the total relationship. Neither black women or black men are free to relate to each other because each is always thinking about what went on in the past.

Black men are more giving of themselves with white women than with black women because they are not so uptight about proving their manhood with white women. Black men can allow more of the inner things to come out and express themselves, whereas with black women they feel too vulnerable because of guilt and they can't open themselves up as much as with a white woman. Black men don't feel the pressure with a white woman, and that is why they can walk to the park, hold hands, and not feel like a sissy or something like that.

R3 is a twenty-year-old sophomore:

There are big problems between black men and black women on this campus. The atmosphere on campus is too "Peyton Place-like." I have made a decision not to go with guys on campus because everything you do becomes a matter of public knowledge. So you get labelled and categorized as being a certain way whether it is true or not.

Some of the guys on campus feel they have a responsibility to get the sisters together in their minds. You know, to make them black. Actually, it is a trick to try to get the girls to go to bed with them. And if the girls don't do it then they are not black. That means you can't be for the strike, the revolution, the community, or black men if you don't come through. The guys use such terms as "sapphire," "mammy maid" [mama's child, country] in order to manipulate black women to do as they want; especially if the girl talks back to them or is not coming through [going to bed].

If a girl did not have a sexual hang-up when she came to campus, the way the guys come on would produce it. Sex is a trip, a game played by the guys. They don't care about black women as persons, but as categories or types. . . . This particular problem is the biggest reason why the black student organization is not as strong as it should be.

[96]

R5 is a nineteen-year-old junior:

Black women on this campus are confused and mindless. They don't know how to relate to the black man. As a consequence they are steady getting fucked over. The black man is fucked up, too, because the woman is not on her job. A man is a product of what the woman puts into him. It's up to her to make a man. . . .

I don't dig the black man running around with white women. If your mind is on blackness and you're running around with a white woman you are fucking up. . . . We're trying to build something and you stand there negating the whole thing.

I've heard black dudes say, "I'm just running a game on the white chicks!" That's a damn lie! You ain't running no game on nobody! If that's what the white chicks want, how in the fuck do you think you're running a game on them? . . . I don't even want to hear rationalizations talking about black women won't come across. No, I won't come across with nothing unless I think it's worth it, and if I see you there with the white girls, you ain't never going to be worth it!

As in the case of the black man, the black movement has generated certain role expectations for the black woman, especially vis-à-vis the black man. Again, however, the mandate is unclear, except for the general notion that her role is to facilitate the black man's becoming a man and thereby to give substance to the concept of black unity.

The black woman realizes that history has cast her in the image of a "castrator" of her black mate's manhood, and that she is still seen in that perspective by the black man. At the same time she is also aware of all that black women have had to go through as a consequence of what society has done to the black man. Yet she has been made to feel that she is to blame for the problem that exists between her and her black man.

Her definition of the black movement is consistent with that given by black men; i.e., she tends to concede that the movement is basically a liberating thrust for the black man, enabling him to capture and assert his manhood. For her the crucial question is how she can best assist in this venture,

[97]

destroy her image as an obstacle to the black man's quest for manhood, and achieve and maintain the feeling of womanhood. With respect to her sexual identity, the question is how she can avoid the feeling (and the reality) of being solely an object of sexual gratification. All of these are real issues for her. They guide how she relates to and defines the movement, black men, and herself. While she admits to the liberating efficacy of the black movement for the black man, she also feels the burden of having to demonstrate to the black man (in the name of black unity and commitment to The Struggle) that she is not the black matriarch and that she wants to help reach the goals of the movement in harmony with the black man.

The legacy of the matriarch inherited by the black woman tends to make her feel that she is to blame for much of the problem. While R5, quoted above, was more vehement and dramatic in her statement than most female respondents, she expresses a theme which runs through statements made by other female respondents. This theme emphasizes that black women see themselves as significant contributors to the black man's problem and to the problem of unity. There is pressure on the black woman, then, to disprove the image imposed upon her; she must prove that she is different from that image of the domineering black matriarch. Basically, this task revolves around her showing deference to the wishes of the black man.

While many black women feel that the black man is reacting to them primarily as personifications—or vestiges— of the black matriarch and only secondarily as mimics of white women and white society, they see the stalemate in their relationship as primarily due to the females aping and accepting white values. R12 says:

> The problem with the black woman is that she doesn't have anything material and she wants everything. Black women are always saying "Do this for me, buy me this, take me here and show me this." This makes it hard for a black man who has nothing to deal with the black woman.

We find this theme in the statements above, especially in

[98]

those of R10, R13, and R28: the theme of black women demanding too much of black men, not being understanding enough, aping the material values of white society. R12 feels that, as a consequence, black men feel pressured and go to white women:

> White women are prepared to take more shit from black men. The black woman has to look out for herself because both the man and herself try to get out of the relationship what they can.
>
> White women can be more loving and understanding toward black men because they have more than the black woman and demand less than she. The white woman has less opportunity and less cause to make black men feel less than men.

This statement brings us back to a consideration of one of the main problems black women have with black men—their relationship with white women. To the black female it is not only a question of jealousy, but also concerns the seriousness of the movement. She becomes suspicious about a man's motives when she sees him rapping "blackness" at one time, and then later walking around with a blonde on his arm or stealing away in the night to share the bed of his white paramour. The consequences complicate an atmosphere already characterized by feelings of distrust, thereby minimizing the opportunity for creating an atmosphere conducive to getting together and speaking to the dimensions of their mutual problems.

Many black women simply feel that the black man is, in general, conditioned to prefer white standards of beauty; so white girls generally look better to them than black girls. The explanations that black men are using the white women for material gain or for other reasons are received as rationalizations.

Some black women, however, have the viewpoint of R25:

> A lot of black men on campus are interested in a variety of girls on campus. They like to experiment with them, but the black woman has her eye on a lasting relationship with somebody. She looks only for a black man. She won't even experiment with

[99]

men of other colors. If the black woman wants to get married it will be with a black man.

In fact, some black women feel that the black man is being used by the white woman, as was dramatically expressed by R5; or, that they are using each other, as expressed by R30:

> White women show how liberal they are by going with black men. They actually use black men to prove their liberalism. What's funny is that the black man thinks he is using her, too. In fact, they both are using each other. White women get black men to prostitute their manhood and their dignity in order that they can prove how liberal they are.

Regardless of who is using whom, the black women in this study do not like the black man-white woman relationship. However, they remain in doubt as to what their role in the movement should be in relation to the black man. Finding this out requires meaningful communications with him. As we indicated, this can only be facilitated in an atmosphere that is free of distrust, suspicion, and alternative relations, prerequisites which are sadly not in evidence on the predominantly white college campus.

Given her resentment towards the black man-white woman relationship, it is understandable that the black sister gets perturbed with the black man when he says that she is not "black" or that she is not committed to the struggle because she shows reluctance about sharing a bed with him. Not only can she point to his relationships with white women as throwing doubt on his "blackness," but she can also point to the fact that most of the work in the black student movement is accomplished by women—black women doing what they can to achieve some semblance of organization but without assuming any roles in conflict with the black man's assertion of himself.

Obviously the task of the black woman is an arduous one. Her efforts to verbalize her quandary to the black man have only compounded the difficulties. He frequently uses these attempts to confirm his point that "she is not ready for the revolution." Invariably an explanation in defense of her feelings elicits the very thing she seeks to prevent—hostility and anger between the two. This type of sensitivity produces the potential for cyclic dimensions which can only perpetuate the problem. (I do not wish to suggest, however, that *all* black male-female relationships are so unpleasant. The range of variety in types of black male-female relationships conforms to all the complexities found on the spectrum of human nature. Yet there are too many observers in our society, including social scientists, who are quick to translate statements about *some* blacks as categorical statements about *all* blacks, especially if the statements are negative or can be used against blacks.)[12]

The implications of the turmoil of the sexes for black unity are obvious. The direction that the problem will take will depend upon two important factors: first, the resolution of the problem will depend upon the kinds of shared, explicit understandings regarding sex roles emanating from the movement; second, of primary importance are the tolerance and respect that each person needs in order to adapt such roles both to individual needs and to the needs of the movement. While rhetoric and "rapping" are important to these dimensions of this task, both have to be nurtured by tolerance and respect.

[12] The problem of making categorical statements about issues of vast complexity and variation in the black community has been examined by Andrew Billingsley in *Black Families in White America* (New Jersey: Prentice-Hall, 1968). One argument that he develops is that scholarly treatment of the black family has tended to obscure more than illuminate the complexities of black family life. He states that while the black family has come in for some scholarship, this attention has been directed to only that "half" of Negro families in the lower class, and even more specifically, that "third" of Negro families below the poverty line, or that "quarter" of Negro families headed by women, or that "tenth" of Negro families with illegitimate children, or that even smaller proportion of Negro families which combine these three conditions and are supported by public welfare (p. 206).

summary and discussion V

By focusing on the politics practiced by black college students at the University of California at Berkeley, I have described a facet of the distressing plight of black college students—especially those on predominantly white campuses. I have given attention to some social, political, and psychological factors emerging from the thrust of the Black Power Movement that have, on one hand, called for unity, yet have ironically militated against the cementing of black unity on these campuses. The black political atmosphere and the white educational setting in which the black student operates have combined to produce two opposing ideals. In this regard I have demonstrated how the sudden interjection of black norms[1] into the campus experience of black students has created for them a condition of role conflict. On the one hand is the preservation of the status quo intrinsically linked with white culture with its illusory rewards of

---

[1] The use of "black norm" here is to be distinguished from the way it is used by Grier and Cobbs in *Black Rage*. These noted black authors use the term to sum up normal adaptive psychological devices that black people have acquired as responses to the conditions of being black in white America:

> We submit that it is necessary for a black man in America to develop a profound distrust of his white fellow citizens and of the nation. He must be on guard to protect himself against cheating, slander, humiliation and outright mistreatment by the official representatives of society. If he does not so protect himself, he will live a life of such pain and shocks as to find life itself unbearable (p. 149).

The sense in which the term "norm" is used in this work is sociological; i.e., norms are a body of shared understandings which are prescribed as guidelines for black behavior, and against which assessments can be made to determine the degree of one's "blackness."

money and position. On the other hand are the counter-values of "blackness"—values which, although not precisely defined, call for black people across the board to unite to celebrate "blackness" and denounce "whiteness." In this context the black college student feels called upon to respond as both a "student" and a black person; however, his very position as a student, which in the pre-Black Power era would have given him credentials of leadership, now forms the base for charges of his having "sold out."

In politics we have examined how a hierarchical scale of "blackness" is used for a variety of purposes, from blacker-than-thou games with the intent of coercion to the purging of guilt feelings. In the area of black male-female relations we have investigated expectations which have aggravated already existing difficulties in the establishment of the kind of wholesome relationships that "blackness" calls for. We must now investigate the meaning of these ingredients of the student's socio-political experience for the Black Student Movement.

To handle these issues in a meaningful way we must first determine the stage of growth of the Black Power version of the Black Student Movement. As such it is still very much in its embryonic stage, still caught in the youthful throes of seeking definitions for itself. However, involved in this effort at definition are problems that, if not treated properly, will issue into the Black Student Movement's having diminishing effectiveness in mobilizing the participation of black students. Two of these problem areas are: (1) the "blacker-than-thou" game, and (2) the problem of black male-female incompatibility. What follows is a brief summation of these two problems and their effects on black unity.

The inherent characteristics of a blacker-than-thou attitude are intolerance and contempt for those who are not as "black" or as "ready" (terms which in this context have the same meaning) as oneself. Such a position frequently has one of two results: (1) if the accused concludes that "blackness" means one either has to take verbal abuse or render it upon other blacks, then he decides that he would rather not deal with it; or (2) if he was intimidated into complying with a certain position, this fact remains utmost in his mind; and as soon as the immediate crisis is over he returns to his former position. In either case the movement has lost a potential recruit. One individual stays long enough to give the impression of unity; the other doesn't. The point is that neither likes the idea of being treated or seeing others treated in a contemptuous way, and the tendency is to move away from such treatment rather than to directly challenge it. The fact, then, that we are hearing black students say "If that is what blackness is all about, later with it" is not simply a rationalization for non-participation (although it is that, too); it is an explanation that also comes from those who have demonstrated concern for problems facing black people.

One can argue on the basis of expediency that blacker-than-thou games have some utility in generating participation in crisis situations; but if people respond by shying away from collective involvement with blacks after the crisis is over, then it is clear that an on-going student organization which attempts to deal methodically with issues and problems will have difficulty in being established. If a student organizational mechanism does not exist on campus, or if such a mechanism can only be approximated through tactics that most black students find intolerable, then it is questionable whether such behavior even conforms to the definition of a movement. As cited in Chapter III, there is evidence that for many black students, participating in "campus unrest" is a cathartic art for demonstrating one's "blackness." Once that purging has been accomplished, students feel they have paid their dues to "blackness" and are then free to go ahead and do their own thing.

Some speculations can be made regarding the collision course of males and females in the Black Student Movement. The possibility of black females taking a more active, public role in organizational affairs appears to be imminent. A growing number of black female students are not as patient as some think they should be in terms of giving their men time to "get themselves together." The combination of tension regarding black men's relationships with white women and the related lack of confidence in the men's commitment to the black movement (plus, perhaps, the effect of the Women's Liberation Movement) will direct black women to assume in a more public fashion some of the tasks they feel the movement requires.

The tension between the sexes on campus may also encourage black females to refrain from romantic entanglements with the black students in favor of black males in the larger community who, the females feel, are not as preoccupied with "manhood" hangups. This would also tend to give their love life a more private character by removing it from the pressures of blacks on campus.

The likelihood of black female students making themselves more available to white males on campus has some foundation. I feel, however, that trends in this direction will be checked by the "turncoat" definition that black female students are inclined to give interracial romances.

Two other subjects concerning the Black Student Movement deserve mention, namely, role conflict and white radicals.

The role conflict expressed on the campus does not operate in a vacuum. It is influenced by and in fact a manifestation of the general conflict found within the more active segments of the black community, where we find antagonism between those blacks who consider themselves "cultural nationalists" and those who consider themselves "revolutionary nationalists." Each group has its army of followers. Recently, the ideologies of these camps have made white participation in the black movement a heated issue between two of the giants in the Black Movement, Eldridge Cleaver and Stokely Carmichael, and have been responsible for Carmichael's terminating his activities with Cleaver and the Black Panther organization. In Southern California this conflict in ideology has led to a continual war between black organizations and to the death of several black people. As long as conflicts of this nature permeate the militant sector of the black community, we can expect problems of uncertainty, antagonism and conflicting roles to trouble the Black Student Movement. However, black students do not

[105]

have to await the resolution of this problem before "getting themselves together." They can initiate solutions by providing a model of togetherness that cuts across seemingly unresolvable differences. Also, because of the luxury of time and the nature of their task as students, they can involve themselves in intellectual endeavors that seek to bring understanding to such issues of the black community.

If role conflict among black students is a product of role conflict in the larger black community, it is also a product of defining the university experience as a white enterprise, and of not doing enough (or not knowing what to do) to facilitate the Black Student Movement or relate to the larger black community in meaningful ways. Thus, for black students, the resolution of role conflict is contingent upon working out definitions that satisfy felt obligations toward the larger black community as well as the demands of student life. Student organizations must not be seen as obstacles to this end, lest the black students on campus end up each "doing his own thing" apart from collective action, or doing nothing.

One of the most common sayings to be heard on campus is "We must return to the community," or "We must relate to the community." If black students understood that there is also a black community on campus that needs to be developed, then much of the energy spent in sermonizing could be used to build strong, cohesive units on campus. "Getting it together" on campus first is an important step to helping the brothers and sisters in "the community" get it together. Too much of the rhetoric directed toward the community is "escapist" in nature—an evasion of the pressing issues of black campus life.

I am reminded of a meeting of approximately two hundred black students. The gathering took place in the church of one of the most highly respected, young, militant ministers in the Bay Area. After sitting quietly through hours of heated debate and hearing students heave verbal abuse upon one another, the minister was asked to make some parting remarks. His remarks can only be paraphrased here:

[106]

I'm not upset about the use of profanity in this church, but what does bother me very much is the extent to which you used it upon each other. In many ways I'm glad that community people were not here to witness this, because you are supposed to be our leaders; you are the ones telling us to get ourselves together. When you come to the community, please do not bring with you the kinds of attitudes and feelings that you have expressed here. We already have enough of that in the community. We in the community will stand behind you all the way, but it is important that you also try to get it together. . . .

The explicit mandate of the minister's statement must be taken as a guideline for action by black college students if their rhetoric about relating to the black community is to have substance.

The second subject deserving of mention here concerns black students and white radicals. Although many black college students have been significantly influenced by the bravado of the Black Panther Party (their style of dress, and especially their oratory), black students have not been influenced by their Marxian analysis of society. Therefore the ties that the Panthers have been able to establish with white radical groups have not been forthcoming between black student organizations and white radicals. The absence of such ties is primarily caused by two factors: the first (and I feel foremost) is the preoccupation of black students with defining "blackness," which precludes the achievement of anything more than the most meager of political ties between their organizations and white radical groups; the second factor is their nervousness about having their actions shared by white people at a time when there is considerable distrust regarding whites' motives—including those of white radicals—in dealing with problems of racism. Ironically, this nervousness has occasionally checked the ability of black students to identify and act upon the racist implications of issues being energetically addressed by white radicals, for example, the problems of ecology and the Vietnam War. In any case, serious consideration of political coalitions with white radicals—and, indeed, certain political activities—will have to await a singular direction given to "blackness."

Finally, then, the Black Power phase of the Black Student Movement is at a critical point in its career. It is at a time when understanding, tolerance, and respect within the ranks must take primacy over such issues as ideology, class, and sex. If black students are going to unite in the ways demanded by the present circumstances, they must find new formulas for dealing with these barriers to unity. They must avoid the dangers of defining "blackness" in a narrow way that not only excludes other black people but also excludes action on pressing issues. What is required at the outset, then, is a definition of "blackness" that elevates the role of understanding, tolerance, and respect, and one that facilitates action against racism.

addendum: "gettin' over"   VI

It is not easy to escape mentally from a concrete situation, to refuse its ideology while continuing to live with its actual relationships. From now on, he [the colonizer who refuses his privileged position] lives his life under the sign of a contradiction which looms at every step, depriving him of all coherence and all tranquility.[1]

For a people who have historically been required to suppress their heritage, the effort to achieve "manhood" in white America and then to accept that most despised part of themselves is an undertaking of great magnitude even under the most benign conditions. Basically this is the problem which confronts the black college student. When the incompatibility of being a black person and being a student was at its height in 1968-69—and even before this—many black students dropped out of school to be more fully involved in the struggle of the black community. Some of these students, such as Huey Newton and Bobby Seale, gained national attention for their efforts in behalf of the black community. But most students remained on campus, and many of these felt the pressure of guilt for having done so. Their commitment to academics and its promises, however, would not allow them to leave the campus; so they stayed and created a disturbance.

But that was in the late sixties. What is happening now and why? Our present vantage point allows us the opportunity to provide some assessment of this question.

1 Albert Memmi, *The Colonizer and the Colonized,* p. 20.

Compelling evidence suggests that at present not much is going on of a political nature among black college students. Indeed, it appears that the atmosphere existing today is quite similar to that which existed prior to the appearance of campus unrest activities; i.e., it appears that black students have come full circle in their political journey. They have come back to a position that places a premium on "college life as usual," i.e., an indifference toward anything other than college activities. Thus, they have returned to a situation of basic isolation from the concerns of the larger black community.

But even here, the entry of drug usage as a serious problem has served to deplete much of the vigor that could be invested in traditional campus activities. The political circle of black students has also become a victim of the drug monster. Two primary factors account for this phenomenon among black students. One of these factors stems from the identity ties that many students are attempting to fashion with certain elements of the larger black community. These students end up over-romanticizing certain destructive activities that they feel link them with the heart of "blackness." Drug usage in this instance not only allows for a psychological identification with the "black experience"; it also, on occasion, provides a physical link with those in the black community who play an active role in sustaining the drug culture. Purchasing drugs from and/or using drugs with these individuals become conspicuous manifestations of student empathy. News of students being "strung out" or hurt in some fashion—especially females—from these "empathetic" relationships are topics of conversation among other black students.

The other factor contributing to drug usage among black college students is much more escapist in nature and national in scope. It consists of the need to escape the frustration of being continually hurt or defeated by unfortunate circumstances of life. Many black students meet such frustrations in their dealings with the white man as they attempt to bring about significant academic and political changes on campus. But, perhaps more immediately, the "escape thesis" speaks to the difficulties that black students have in their relationships with fellow black students. The issue of going through "changes" with the opposite sex, the frustrations of getting one's self and others together in a "black" political way, the problem of continual "fronting" to be accepted, etc. are among the experiences whose intensity often occasions the need to escape. For this, drugs are a convenient and available vehicle.

The prominence of the drug problem is germane to the existence of the "ante bellum status quo" within the sociopolitical world of black college students. This is so because drugs sap energies that have political potential, and because the general consequences of drug use are to hold individuals fast to the complications of their individual problem. There are, however, two other factors contributing to this status quo that are worthy of our consideration.

One of these factors is social control. It is difficult to minimize the importance of the techniques available to the establishment for quieting student activities and maintaining their silence. There is the highly visible repressive role of the police—shootings, head-bangings, etc.; there is the procedure for dismissal of those identified with unrest activities; and there is the reality of students having their financial support taken away for involvement in activities displeasing to the administration. When one considers that a substantial number of black students come to college under some federally supported program, it becomes easier to understand why they have cooled their "revolutionary" activities. Another aspect of social control is the internalizing by many black students of a definition of college life that precludes any political activities designed to change the traditional image of the university. These various types of social control, then, are powerful factors in explaining the political silence of black students on campus. Perhaps even more demanding of emphasis, however, is an increasingly influential climate within the black students' socio-political world. Though I do not suggest that all—or even most—black college students fall within the purview of this climate, nonetheless its influence among black students is both substantial and growing.

[111]

A term that is frequently used among black college students is that of "gettin' over." They normally use the term to refer to how one is doing in a particular course. "Gettin' over" suggests that the individual is meeting at least the minimum requirements of the course with a minimal amount of effort and commitment. In these pages, I use the term "gettin' over" to designate a philosophy—a way of viewing the world and coming to terms with it. At the heart of this philosophy of "gettin' over" are two important elements: the first element is a highly individualistic orientation—an overriding concern for self. The other element is the *use* of "blackness" to achieve the specific objective of the individual. For the most part the philosophy is closely related to that of the "blackness pimps" discussed in Chapter II, without the active blacker-than-thou political context. This philosophy is particularly evident in the classroom.

For a number of black students the appearance of black studies courses was seen as a blessed event for their own ends; i.e., the courses could be used as a device to get through school with a modicum of endeavor. In the first place, many students with this point of view feel they already know all there is to know about black people, and though they sign up for black studies courses they feel no compelling need to attend classes. Ironically, in many of these courses that also have white students in the class, one finds that the white students are more serious about the academic aspects of the black experience than many of the black students taking the course. For the professor, especially if he is black, it is disconcerting to have white students at the forefront of the class and to have the bulk of the better grades go to them. More often than not, such a situation is the result of black students' not being seriously committed to expanding their understanding of the black experience as a prerequisite for informed action in the black populace.

Secondly, if such a course requires extensive reading and/or writing of papers, many of the students will argue vehemently that doing so is a "white man's thing," and that blacks are an "oral people." Notwithstanding the merit of

[112]

blacks as an "oral people," the argument is most frequently used to avoid doing any work for the course. (Many of these same students, however, will be found working arduously for a grade in a "white studies" course given by a white professor!) Often in lieu of doing research requiring reading and/or writing, the argument will surface that "I'm working out in the community, and I should get a grade for that rather than being graded for all that academic bullshit." What these students have been doing in the community, how their activities relate to the course, how they have benefited from the experience—indeed, whether they have in fact done anything at all in the community—are all questions that they feel are covered by the declaration that they have been "working in the community," or that "I was in the movement and I got my ass busted so you [instructor] could get this job. Now you talkin' the white.man's grade shit. Man, you benefitin' from my action. You wasn't even there when the shit came down."

If a white instructor is teaching a black studies course or a course that is heavily weighted toward some aspect of the black experience, black students frequently seize the opportunity to intimidate him into giving them good grades. Their intimidation takes the form of suggesting that he is a racist or that his interpretations are racist. As has been noted earlier, most whites do not like to be called racist; so at times they will go to great lengths to counter the label—including the awarding of grades that are not deserved, especially to students whose outspokenness threatens them. For the teacher it is no big problem to give such grades. But the student receiving good grades through these means has his tactics reinforced as a way of negotiating future courses.

Black professors do not entirely escape such tactics. Many students have the notion that black studies were established to enable them to get through the white man's academic system. These students also assume that this is implicitly understood by the black teachers. Black teachers who do not make it easy for black students are viewed by them as causing a breach in the mutual trust, and as being not "ready." A personal acquaintance relates that he was

[113]

able to get his department to establish a course in which he could spend time with those black students having trouble understanding some of the theories and concepts in the field. The course was designed to allow for a maximum of give and take between the students on particular issues in the black experience without the problem of white attendance. He recounts that about an hour before the first class meeting, one of the young women who signed up for the course approached him. She told him that she would not be able to attend the class that day because of an appointment at the beauty shop. She further indicated that she would not be able to attend very many of his classes because she was graduating at the end of the year and had to study hard for other courses. Finally she let him know that she was, however, expecting an A in the course!

I understand that this concern to get through a course and to graduate from college, as well as the off-hand measures often employed to do so, are not a monopoly of black students. White fraternities, especially, have long been famous for the systematic unethical ways used to get their members through college. File cabinets in fraternity houses are crammed with questions and answers from past examinations, and course papers are bandied about within the membership. In addition, frat brothers who are teaching associates frequently encourage other frat members to take the course they assist in order to insure an easy grade. Nor am I unaware of the degree to which the system itself generates these kinds of maneuvers by its emphasis on the almighty grade. But what is of concern here is the manner in which the concept of "blackness" has been exploited by some students as an instrument to satisfy their academic interests. For these students, "revolution by any means necessary" has been replaced by "a grade by any means necessary—except, perhaps, by studying."

The "gettin' over" philosophy coupled with the artificial adoption of black lower-class values on the campus raises some crucial questions about the black student's commitment. It would appear that notwithstanding the revolutionary clichés that undergirded their earlier demonstrations and strikes there is a growing sense of well-being among the students regarding the accommodations provided them by the university, with the result that there is no longer the compelling need to be involved in the protracted struggle they had defined for the black community. There is instead a return to the assimilationist-integrationist status quo of traditional student life.

The impact of the "gettin' over" philosophy can also be seen in relationships between black male and black female students. An attitude best described as "who is going to screw over who first?" has become a guideline governing the approach that each takes to the opposite sex. There is an implicit understanding that one (or both) is destined to be hurt by the other. It is also understood that each relationship is temporary, and the object therefore is to get out of it as much as possible without giving too much. The critical question in establishing a relationship is, "What can you do for me?" While both sexes have this question in mind, the attitude appears to be more characteristic of men than women. Several factors allow black men to assume this stance with more frequency than women: the movement for men to assert their manhood, the availability of white women, and the relative shortage of black men. There is a feeling of confidence generally shared by men—not shared generally by women—that they do not have to put up with anything less than what they want. There are "too many fish in the sea" from which they can choose. Because black women are aware of this situation, they frequently have to play games to attract men; and because of the competition, they play games to keep them. The continuing uncertainty about "real" feelings makes it difficult to establish warm or lasting relationships, and the expectation of being hurt becomes a self-fulfilling prophecy. The intensity of these concerns tends to relegate other issues—e.g., politics, academics—to at best a secondary consideration.

The foregoing discussion of present trends suggests the need for refocusing the question of what the period of black student unrest in the late sixties really meant. It would appear that the theory viewing the black student as caught between the pull of two antithetical poles (values of the middle class and values of "blackness") was basically describing a situational conflict; i.e., the internal tension felt by students with the appearance of Black Power disappeared along with the dissipation on the national level of the emotions brought forth by the slogan. Now it seems that the middle-class values that were temporarily suppressed have again moved to center stage in their influence on black students' attitudes, although they are frequently cloaked in black lower-class trappings. Apparently, the "revolutionary" experience of the black students was primarily an emotional reaction to the abruptness of the challenge of "blackness," and a preoccupation with adjusting to it psychologically. Commitment to a radical transformation of institutions of higher learning was a symptom of this preoccupation, rather than a goal in itself. The activities of campus unrest were more symbolic than demonstrations of a real concern. The psychological effect of these symbolic activities, at that time, for the quest for manhood and the assertion of "blackness," was profound. From this perspective, then, black student unrest was primarily a cathartic act allowing for the expenditure of intense emotions of guilt, conflict, and frustration. Having expanded these emotional energies and paid their dues, many black students now continue their search for the proverbial piece of the pie. This time they are stocked with the trappings of blackness that can be used to "get them over"—individually.

The remaining impression is that despite all the political rhetoric and alleged political consciousness, and despite the fact that black college students have consciously rejected the superficial marks of what Frazier relentlessly exposed in *Black Bourgeoisie,* students appear to view the world no differently than their counterparts of ten or twenty years ago. If this charge is accurate, it gives a ringing plausibility to the notion of the "black anglo-saxon."[2] Moreover, it

2 The term "black anglo-saxon" was first brought to my attention through Nathan Hare's book, *The Black Anglo-Saxons* (New York: Marzani & Munsell, 1965). The author says in his foreword:
Black Anglo-Saxons are chiefly distinguishable in that, in their struggle to

raises again all the issues that many thought were being put to rest with the manifestation of the Black Power Movement, i.e., the problem of individualism and indifference toward the plight of the black masses. Obviously, if this is the case, then it is clear that the name of the game has not changed; only the rhetoric has.

To have one's "blackness" challenged today does not elicit the same defensive emotional response it did three years ago; nor will black students go to the same lengths they once did to prove their "blackness." Yet students are still concerned about having their "blackness" questioned. This concern tends to make them overly cautious about what they say or do until they receive (or feel they will receive) substantial feedback endorsing their act. For example, in the classroom there are occasions when black students and black professors have questions they would like to raise or statements they would like to make, but the uncertainty about the "blackness" of the question or statement causes them to withhold their participation. Initiative, creativity, and criticism are therefore stifled. Or, if the instructor is understood to have a certain black ideology that may be different from their own (Pan-Africanism, cultural nationalism, revolutionary nationalism, etc.), the tendency is for the students to "right on" the teacher, to mimic the teacher's ideology in their papers or exams, and to shy away from critically examining either the teacher's ideology or their own. "Blackness" of this nature becomes a restrictive, rubber-stamping, follow-the-leader kind of experience, rather than a mind-expanding, issue-oriented experience geared to providing students with the wherewithal to contribute to the development of self and community.

Fighting the detrimental effects of the "out-blacking" and "gettin' over" gestures depends on the black students' acceptance of the fact that the black community needs the intellectual input of its progeny for its own wholesome

---

throw off the smothering blanket of social inferiority, they disown their own history and mores in order to assume that of the biological descendants of the white Anglo-Saxons. They relate to, and long to be part of, the elusive and hostile white world, whose norms are taken as models of behavior.

[117]

development. One's active commitment to some of the problems among the black citizenry is ultimately more important than one's present political ideology; for one's ideology is far more subject to change than are the needs of the community. The fact that black college students have the time to identify, debate, and to take action on pressing community issues is a luxury to be taken advantage of. For the most part the student is subsidized to take part in this enterprise of learning about the world and creating ways of handling some of its problems. It is clear, then, that this is not the time to apologize for being a student. Apologizing will not facilitate the development of young black minds; nor will it bring the collective strengths of these minds to bear upon the ills of the black community. Apologizing only issues into intellectual footshuffling and paralysis of action. The gravity of the black experience is too great to allow for another generation of black heirs to engage in such self-indulgent exercises. The mandate for black college students is to be consciously aware of the predicament of the black community, and to seize every opportunity to advance its struggle for freedom and justice.

appendix

Profile of Respondents

R1 — Male; 27-year-old graduate student in Sociology; born in Mississippi. Has been on campus one year. Plans to teach and do research upon completion of studies.

R2 — Male; 29-year-old graduate student in History; born in Alabama. Has been on campus five years. Plans to teach upon completion of studies.

R3 — Female; 20-year-old sophomore in Humanities; born in California. Has been on campus one year and a half. Plans to teach. Has 3.2 grade point average.[1]

R4 — Female; 27-year-old senior in Social Sciences; born in Florida. Has been on campus one year. Plans to teach. Has 3.7 grade point average.

R5 — Female; 19-year-old junior in Social Sciences; born in Texas. Has been on campus two years. Plans to teach. Has 3.5 grade point average.

R6 — Male; 30-year-old graduate student in Social Welfare; born in Texas. Has been on campus for two years. Plans to have private practice in psychiatry.

R7 — Female; 29-year-old graduate student in Folklore; born in New York. Has been on campus for two years. Plans to write books for black children.

[1] Grade point averages are based on a four point scale at the University of California. Grade point averages of graduate students are not indicated.

R8 — Male; 24-year-old senior. Has independent field major; born in Kentucky. Has been on campus for three years. Plans to write and be involved in politics. Has 3.4 grade point average.

R9 — Male; 19-year-old sophomore in Pre-med; born in Texas. Has been on campus one year. Plans to be children's heart specialist. Has 2.0 grade point average.

R10— Female; 21-year-old senior in Anthropology; born in California. Has been on campus three years. Plans to teach. Has 3.8 grade point average.

R11— Male; 18-year-old sophomore in Anthropology; born in Illinois. Has been on campus one year. Plans to teach and do research. Has 2.2 grade point average.

R12— Female; 21-year-old senior in Sociology; born in California. Has been on campus four years. Undecided about occupation. Has 3.0 grade point average.

R13— Female; 20-year-old junior in Sociology; born in Washington, D. C. Has been on campus two years. Plans to teach. Has 3.0 grade point average.

R14— Male; 30-year-old graduate student in Sociology; born in Michigan. Has been on campus one year. Plans to teach.

R15— Female; 26-year-old graduate student in Social Welfare; born in California. Has been on campus one year. Plans to be a high school counselor.

R16— Male; 20-year-old junior in History; born in New York. Has been on campus one year and a half. Plans to be medical doctor. Has 3.8 grade point average.

R17— Male; 21-year-old senior in Political Science; born in California. Has been on campus three years. Plans to be an attorney. Has 2.9 grade point average.

R18— Female; 24-year-old senior in History; born in Washington. Has been on campus three years. Plans to teach. Has 2.8 grade point average.

[120]

R19— Male; 30-year-old graduate student in Sociology; born in Alabama. Has been on campus two years. Plans to teach.

R20— Female; 22-year-old senior in Political Science; born in California. Has been on campus two years. Plans to be an actress. Has 3.0 grade point average.

R21— Female; 20-year-old junior in English; born in California. Has been on campus two years. Plans to teach. Has 3.6 grade point average.

R22— Male; 19-year-old junior in Sociology; born in Alabama. Has been on campus two years. Undecided about occupation. Has 2.5 grade point average.

R23— Male; 22-year-old junior in Political Science; born in New York. Has been on campus two years. Plans to be an attorney. Has 3.5 grade point average.

R24— Male; 26-year-old graduate student in History; born in Illinois. Has been on campus two years. Plans to teach.

R25— Female; 22-year-old senior in Philosophy; born in California. Has been on campus two years. Plans to teach. Has 3.0 grade point average.

R26— Male; 21-year-old sophomore. Undeclared major; born in Washington, D. C. Has been on campus one year. Plans to teach. Has 2.0 grade point average.

R27— Male; 22-year-old senior in Social Science; born in California. Has been on campus four years. Plans to be high school counselor. Has 2.7 grade point average.

R28— Female; 26-year-old graduate student in Counseling Psychology; born in Tennessee. Has been on campus one year and a half. Undecided about occupation.

R29— Male; 23-year-old senior in Rhetoric; born in California. Has been on campus four years. Undecided about occupation. Has 2.2 grade point average.

[121]

R30— Male; 29-year-old sophomore. Undeclared major; born in California. Has been on campus a year and a half. Undecided about occupation. Has 2.9 grade point average.

R31— Male; 29-year-old graduate student in English; born in Georgia. Has been on campus two and a half years. Plans to teach.

R32— Male; 20-year-old junior in Political Science; born in Mississippi. Has been on campus a year and a half. Plans to be an attorney. Has 3.0 grade point average.

R33— Male; 23-year-old graduate student in Political Science; born in Louisiana. Has been on campus three years. Undecided about occupation.

R34— Male; 22-year-old senior in Social Science; born in New York. Has been on campus two years. Undecided about occupation. Has 2.7 grade point average.

R35— Female; 21-year-old senior in Anthropology; born in California. Has been on campus a year and a half. Plans to teach. Has 3.5 grade point average.

R36— Female; 20-year-old sophomore in Mathematics; born in California. Has been on campus a year and a half. Plans to teach. Has 2.3 grade point average.

R37— Male; 29-year-old senior in Political Science; born in Texas. Has been on campus two and a half years. Plans to teach. Has 3.0 grade point average.

R38— Male; 19-year-old sophomore in Engineering; born in California. Has been on campus a year and a half. Plans to be electronics engineer. Has 2.0 grade point average.

R39— Male; 21-year-old senior in Political Science; born in Texas. Has been on campus three and a half years. Plans to teach. Has 2.7 grade point average.

R40— Female; 20-year-old sophomore. Undeclared major; born in California. Has been on campus a year and a half. Undecided about occupation. Has 2.4 grade point average.

bibliography

Bell, Inge Powell. *CORE and the Strategy of Nonviolence.* New York: Random House, 1968.

Billingsley, Andrew. *Black Families in White America.* New Jersey: Prentice-Hall, 1968.

Blauner, Robert. "Internal Colonialism and Ghetto Revolt," *Social Problems,* XVI, No. 4 (Spring 1969).

Blumer, Herbert. *Symbolic Interactionism: Perspective and Method.* New Jersey: Prentice-Hall, 1969.

Breitman, George (ed.). *Malcolm X Speaks.* New York: Grove Press, 1966.

Brockriede, Wayne and Robert L. Scott. *The Rhetoric of Black Power.* New York: Harper & Row, 1969.

Carmichael, Stokely. "Power and Racism," *The Black Power Revolt.* Floyd Barbour (ed.). Toronto: Macmillan, 1968.

Carmichael, Stokely and Charles V. Hamilton. *Black Power: The Politics of Liberation in America.* New York: Random House, 1967.

Clark, Kenneth B. *Dark Ghetto.* New York: Harper & Row, 1965.

Cleaver, Eldridge. *Soul on Ice.* New York: Dell, 1968.

Cobbs, Price M. and William H. Grier. *Black Rage.* New York: Bantam Books, 1968.

Dubois, W. E. B. *The Souls of Black Folks.* New York: Fawcett World Library, 1965.

Elkins, Stanley. *Slavery.* Chicago: University of Chicago Press, 1959.

Essien-Udom, E. U. *Black Nationalism: The Search for an Identity.* Chicago: University of Chicago Press, 1962.

Frazier, E. Franklin. *Black Bourgeoisie: The Rise of a New Middle Class in the United States.* Glencoe, Illinois: Free Press, 1957.

———. *On Race Relations.* Chicago: University of Chicago Press, 1968.

———. *The Negro Family in the United States.* Chicago: University of Chicago Press, 1939.

Getzels, J. E. and E. G. Guba. "Role, Role Conflict and Effectiveness: An Empirical Study," *American Sociological Review,* XIX (1954).

Hare, Nathan. *The Black Anglo-Saxons.* New York: Marzani & Munsell, 1965.

Hernton, Calvin C. *Sex and Racism in America.* New York: Grove Press, 1968.

Kahn, Tom. "Problems of the Negro Movement," *Problems and Prospects of the Negro Movement.* Raymond J. Murphy and Howard Elinson (eds.). Belmont, California: Wadsworth, 1966.

Key, V. O., Jr. *Politics, Parties and Pressure Groups.* New York: Thomas Y. Crowell, 1964.

Lee, Don L. *Don't Cry, Scream.* Detroit: Broadside Press, 1969.

———. *We Walk the Way of The New World.* Detroit: Broadside Press, 1970.

Lomax, Louis. *Negro Revolt.* New York: Harper & Row, 1963.

Meier, August. "In Protest Movements and Organizations," *Journal of Negro Education,* XXXII (1963).

Memmi, Albert. *The Colonizer and the Colonized.* Boston: Beacon Press, 1967.

Poussaint, Alvin and Linda McLean. "Black Roadblocks to Black Unity," *Negro Digest,* XVII (November 1968).

Roszak, Theodore. *The Making of a Counter Culture.* Garden City, New York: Doubleday, 1969.

Schwartz, Morris R. and Charlotte Green Schwartz. "Problems in Participant Observation," *American Journal of Sociology,* LX (January 1955).

Stampp, Kenneth. *The Peculiar Institution.* New York: Random House, 1956.

Documents

"Proposal for Establishing a Black Students Department," submitted by the Afro-American Students Union, University of California, Spring 1968.

Report of the National Advisory Commission on Civil Disorder. New York: Bantam Books, 1968.